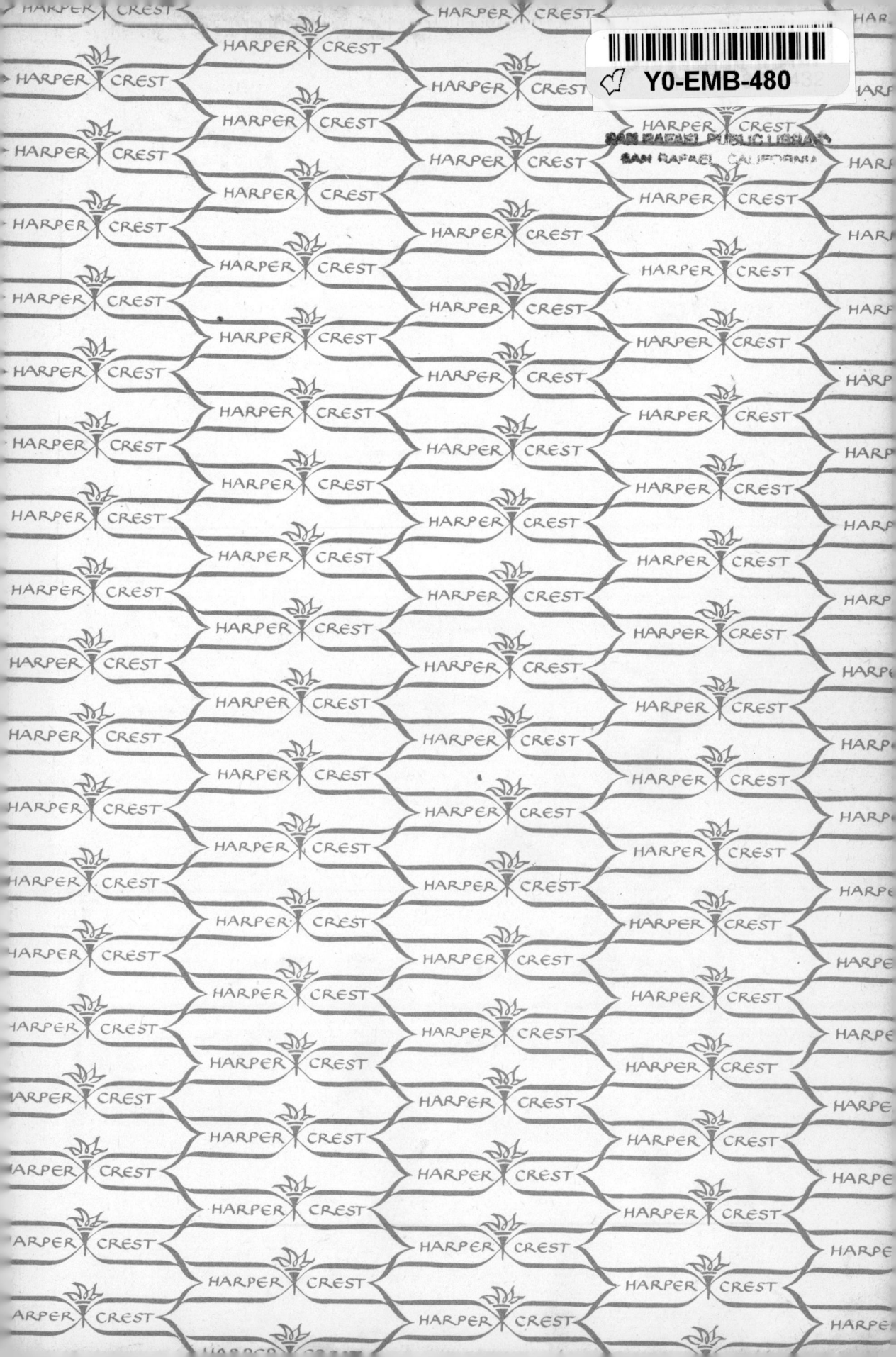

HARPER CREST

NELSON

AND THE AGE OF FIGHTING SAIL

There are six new HORIZON CARAVEL BOOKS
published each year. The titles now available are:

NELSON AND THE AGE OF FIGHTING SAIL
ALEXANDER THE GREAT
RUSSIA UNDER THE CZARS
HEROES OF POLAR EXPLORATION
KNIGHTS OF THE CRUSADES

COVER: *The Battle of Cape St. Vincent is used as a backdrop for a portrait of Nelson.*
VERSAILLES MUSEUM
END SHEETS: *This 1807 painting depicts five ships on which Nelson served. From left to
right are the* Agamemnon, *the* Vanguard, *the* Elephant, *the* Captain, *and the* Victory.
NATIONAL MARITIME MUSEUM
TITLE PAGE: *Sailors sit aloft along a ship's yardarm while they roll up the foresail.*
FRANKLIN D. ROOSEVELT LIBRARY

A HORIZON CARAVEL BOOK

NELSON

AND THE AGE OF FIGHTING SAIL

By the Editors of
HORIZON MAGAZINE

Author
OLIVER WARNER

Consultant
FLEET ADMIRAL CHESTER W. NIMITZ, U.S.N.

ILLUSTRATED WITH PAINTINGS, DRAWINGS,
LETTERS, AND MAPS OF THE PERIOD

Published by American Heritage Publishing Co., Inc.
Book trade distribution by Meredith Press
Institutional distribution by Harper & Row, Publishers

FIRST EDITION
Library of Congress Catalogue Card Number 63-19065
© 1963 by American Heritage Publishing Co., Inc. 551 Fifth Avenue, New York 17,
New York. All rights reserved under Berne and Pan-American Copyright Con-
ventions. U.S. copyright is not claimed for color plates on pages 17 and 106.

Naval Achievements of Great Britain. JENKINS, 1817

FOREWORD

The brief, brilliant career of a young admiral would doubtless have appealed to the people of any patriotic nation in any era. But to the English of the early nineteenth century Horatio Nelson seemed an ideal personality. When he died at Trafalgar at the age of forty-seven, he had become the greatest figure of England's naval history, the most spectacular officer of that age in which sailing ships were at their fighting best.

England in the 1800's desperately needed a man who could win battles against Napoleon's forces—and who could then receive praise and affection warmly. Nelson could do both superlatively; and with his empty sleeve, his blind eye, and his scarred forehead, he even looked the hero. In a romantic age, Nelson was romanticized in art as few men before or since have been.

The background of a Nelson portrait is almost as compelling as the man himself. Artists of the eighteenth and early nineteenth centuries freely substituted new scenes as the careers of their illustrious subjects changed. Art was made to serve the purposes of journalism and publicity as well as grander uses.

Many of the illustrations in this book, portraits and battle scenes, were drawn not long after the smoke had cleared away and the ships had been brought back to port. Some were done by men who served alongside Nelson; others were painted by men who never left England, the artists piecing together a whole picture from firsthand accounts and thirdhand rumors. A few are now nearly as well known as Nelson himself, having carried the fame of their subject all over the world in countless engravings and reproductions.

Nelson has indeed become something more than an isolated figure in a distant time. Because of the universal appeal of his heroic story and the excitement of the art that has kept him in view, Nelson will be remembered as long as men fight on the sea.

—THE EDITORS

NATIONAL MARITIME MUSEUM

Nelson and Trafalgar are represented in this snuff-box portrait.

Moments before victory at the Battle of Cape St. Vincent in 1797, the flagship of the British fleet, at left, exchanges broadsides with a Spaniard.

Sailors on the deck of an embattled British ship "fight" a cannon in this 1784 drawing. About seven men were needed to load, fire, and clean a gun.

CONTENTS

I

BAPTISM OF FIRE

Horatio Nelson first came under fire when he was sixteen. It was Sunday, February 19, 1775, and he was serving as a midshipman in the *Seahorse*, a frigate in the navy of Great Britain's King George III.

An enemy vessel was sighted by the *Seahorse*'s lookout on a voyage in Indian waters between Madras and Bombay. Britain was not at that moment officially at war with her traditional enemy, France; the fast-sailing ship was part of the fleet of a rebel Indian ruler, Hyder Ali. But the French were determined to gain control of the long-distance trade routes that the British were securing all across the world, and France had taken advantage of the difficulties the British were having in conquering India to ally themselves with the ruthless Hyder Ali.

The captain of the *Seahorse* immediately gave chase. He ordered more sail put on his 20-gun frigate and prepared for battle. Captain Farmer was a disciplinarian who expected his men to obey him without question. Nelson had understood this from the moment the ship sailed from England. By the time he finally left the *Seahorse*, the young midshipman had seen the frigate's first lieutenant court-martialed, and no fewer than two hundred times he had seen men lashed with a cat-o'-nine-tails.

The two ships at length drew close to each other—then both opened fire. For a while the contest was brisk; the *Seahorse* fired more than a hundred rounds. And then suddenly it was all over; the Indian vessel surrendered. Midshipman Nelson, who would become the most brilliant figure of the age of sail, had had his baptism of fire.

The midshipman was a slight, fair-haired youngster, less than the average height for his sixteen years. He used the nasal speech of the English county of Norfolk, his birthplace. And when he thought of home, it was of the parsonage at Burnham Thorpe, a village that still stands behind the sand dunes on England's eastern coast. From

A first-rate British warship, with three tiers of cannon exposed on her high sides, is taking aboard supplies in this painting by J. M. W. Turner.

*Nelson's first captain was his
uncle, Maurice Suckling (below);
his first foe, Hyder Ali (above).*

NATIONAL MARITIME MUSEUM

*Nelson's mother died before he ever
went to sea; nevertheless, it was
inevitable that an artist should
paint a sentimental scene of him
bidding farewell to her (right).*

these dunes Nelson as a small boy, standing with his play-mates or numerous brothers and sisters, could look out over the North Sea. There was a great variety of sailing vessels plying the coast, there was the whistle of the wind over the steel-gray waters, and there was the ever-present lure of the sea.

Nelson succumbed to that lure early. When he was short of thirteen, in the year 1771, he secured a berth in His Majesty's Ship *Raisonable* of 64 guns, commanded by his uncle, Captain Maurice Suckling. The boy's reasons for leaving home so young were many, but chief among them was the size of the Nelson family: there were eight sur-viving children, and when Horatio was nine, his mother died. He did not wish to be a burden on his clergyman father any longer than was necessary; in those demanding years of the late eighteenth century many children were working long hours by the time they were his age. Another reason for Nelson's going to sea in 1771 was that his coun-try was then making preparations for a war over the Falk-land Islands, a distant possession of her empire. The war scare eventually died down: Spain and France withdrew their claims to those wind-swept islands off the tip of South America which Britain considered properly hers. The *Raisonable* was one of the successful arguments England had used to defend her ownership, and Captain Suckling had relished the prospect of combat. "Let him [Horatio] come," Suckling wrote, "and the first time we get into action a cannon ball may knock off his head and provide for him."

Above is Nelson's childhood home, the picturesque parsonage house and gar-dens at Burnham Thorpe in Norfolk. His father was rector of the village.

But Nelson's first whiff of grapeshot four years later aboard the *Seahorse* by no means put him out of action. For in the course of those four years that led up to the fight in the Indian Ocean, he had had enough adventures to help him stand up confidently to the test. After his first year on his uncle's ship, he had taken the advice of that kindly old seaman and served a term in the merchant marine, voyaging to the West Indies. He had then returned to the navy and become a midshipman in H.M.S. *Triumph*. But his most exciting time in those early days was aboard the *Carcass*, which took part in a two-ship expedition to the Arctic Circle in 1773.

Although the expedition failed to near the Pole, it got within 600 miles of it, which was a record for that time. And one night, when the ships were frozen in the Arctic ice, Nelson showed some of his characteristic reckless courage. He and a companion evaded the ship's guard and set off across the ice in pursuit of a polar bear. When they were missed, a signal was made to recall them, but Nelson ignored it. He kept on after the bear even though his musket had misfired and his ammunition was all gone. Only when the bear was scared away by a gun fired from the *Carcass* did Nelson return—to receive a severe reprimand.

With such youthful escapades behind him, Nelson doubtless considered himself ready for more significant action. Yet just a year after the brush with Hyder Ali, Nelson's luck seemed to have deserted him. He came down with fever and was invalided home, while the *Seahorse* went on to Malaya and China. He was given passage in the *Dolphin*, a frigate which had already been around the world twice on voyages of exploration. Her captain's name was Pigot, and his care and kindness saved Nelson's life. At first, as the ship rolled her way toward the shores of England, Nelson was dejected.

"I felt impressed with a feeling that I should never rise in my profession," he confessed later. "My mind was staggered with a view of the difficulties I had to surmount, and the little interest [influence] I possessed. I could discern no means of reaching the object of my ambition."

In his feverish condition, his mind reeled through a long and gloomy reverie. He wished he would fall overboard and drown; he became increasingly certain that the navy held no future for him. Yet he dreamed ceaselessly of his career.

The navy that he served was a close-knit service. It was in decline from its peak of greatness in the Seven Years'

Nelson, fourteen, attacks a ferocious polar bear while on a North Pole expedition in July, 1773. A gun was fired from his ship, the Carcass, at the left, which frightened away the bear and probably saved Nelson's life.

15

War (1756–63), when England was allied with Prussia against France and Austria. Nevertheless it still had more prestige than the army, and it was ruled by the small, professional Board of Admiralty to which King George delegated powers of command. The aim of an ambitious midshipman such as Nelson, whose eager spirit belied his frail constitution, was to be made a lieutenant as soon as possible. There was sea time to be served, an examination to pass, and a patron to be sought before he could aspire to an officer's uniform. Once the first hurdles were passed, a lieutenant's best hope was a war. There was the intermittent struggle with France, which was fought not only in European waters but on most of the world's seven seas. And there was soon to be combat with another formidable enemy: Great Britain's American colonies were rising against her in a war for independence. They were to be helped first by France and then by Spain, another power whose world interests clashed with those of Britain.

The Board of Admiralty in London conferred in this paneled office.

TEXT CONTINUED ON PAGE 21

King George III (left) ruled Great Britain during most of Nelson's life. Above are detailed views of a ship of the Georgian navy; the figurehead attached to the bow at left probably represents George III.

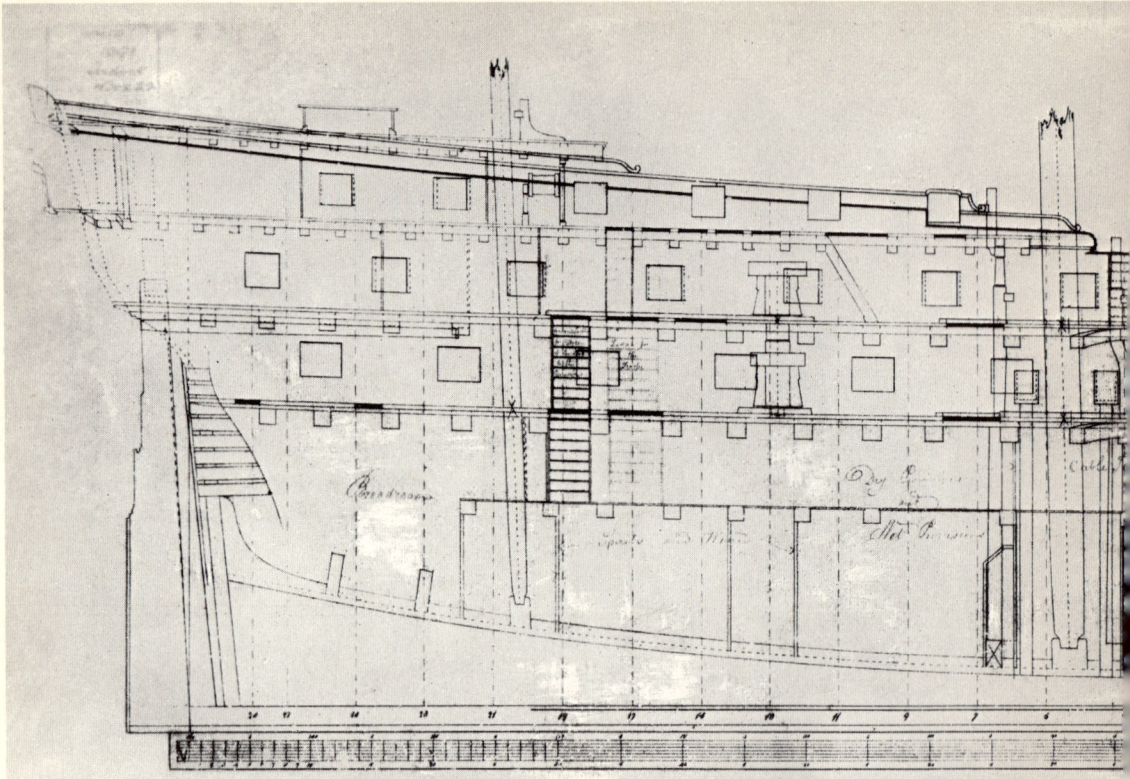

The construction drawing above showed shipwrights how to build Nelson's Agamemnon. The frame of the 64-gun ship was made of oak trees that had grown in English forests for at least a hundred years. She measured 160 feet from stem to stern and displaced 1,376 tons. When launched, half of her deep hull rode underwater.

Below is a cutaway drawing of a two-deck French warship similar to the British type. At the stern, left, are the dining rooms and cabins of the captain and the officers; below and forward of these are storage rooms. In the bow are the galley and the crew's quarters and mess. Amidships, above the horse stalls, is the prison.

One of Nelson's first ships was the **Boreas**, at top left. She patrolled the waters in the West Indies and is shown here with a French frigate. A favorite subject of cartoonists of the time was the "press gang" (bottom left). The state of the navy was so bad that in order to staff a ship, seamen were sent out to drag away citizens.

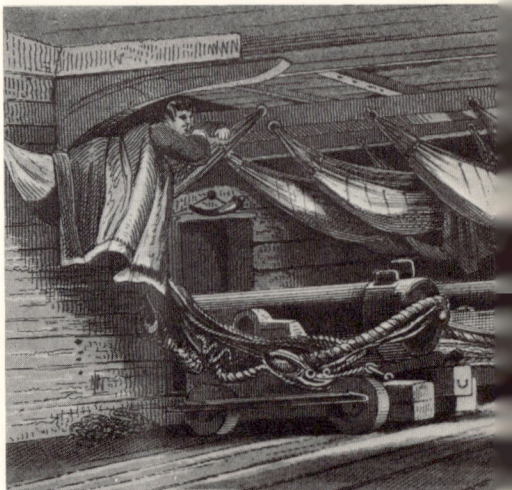

TEXT CONTINUED FROM PAGE 16

By means of a war with these enemies, or by other, slower means, a British naval lieutenant hoped to rise to the rank of commander, then to full, or post, captain. When the rank of post captain was reached, an officer could consider himself a "made man." On active service he would be in charge of a ship of not less than 20 guns; he would have the lion's share of any prize money his enterprise might gather in, and as nothing ever disturbed the rule of seniority among the captains, he had only to live long enough and one day he would become an admiral. Sometimes it was a long wait; hence the need for quick promotion in the earlier stages. A few lucky admirals might find themselves in charge of fleets or squadrons when they themselves were in full vigor.

Navy life for those who were not officers was considerably less promising. The common sailors led a life that few people today would consider possible to bear. Generally they were split up into two groups: those who tended to the ship itself, and those who fought by the guns and manned the rigging.

The men who worked the ships were a mixed lot. Some came to sea and to their dangerous livelihood quite unwillingly. But there were a few volunteers, men who made the navy their life in the same way as the officers. They were mostly skilled, professional seamen: the quartermasters, who were responsible for steering; the ropemakers, carpenters, armorers; the coopers, who looked after the barrels in which water, powder, and stores were kept; the caulkers, who saw to the seams between the planks, which were sealed with tar; and the sailmakers, signalmen, and cooks.

Except for the marines (who formed a corps of waterborne soldiers), the men who fired the guns and managed the sails and rigging were drawn from every possible source. They were taken off merchant ships when the navy was shorthanded (as it always was in war), often near home after a weary voyage. They were sometimes "pressed" into service; that is, seized in the ports and forced aboard at the point of a cutlass. They were picked up in foreign ports; for instance, the *Victory*, the great man-of-war Nelson commanded at the peak of his career, carried some 800 officers and men, over 70 of whom were foreigners drawn from

TEXT CONTINUED ON PAGE 24

Lack of comfort was part of a seaman's life. Sailors' hammocks were slung low over the cannons at night, but during the daytime they were rolled up against the sides of the ship to stop flying splinters of gunshot.

OVERLEAF: *Although it was inefficient and corrupt, the Georgian navy could fight. Victor in the famous Battle of the First of June (1794) was Lord Howe, whose dismasted flagship is shown between two French warships.*

GREENWICH HOSPITAL COLLECTION

TEXT CONTINUED FROM PAGE 21

nearly every nationality, including 22 Americans and 3 Frenchmen. Only one man in ten was over forty years old, the vast proportion being between twenty and thirty. The youngest member of the *Victory*'s crew was but ten years old.

The early nineteenth century was a far tougher age than our own, and those who lived to manhood were made of sturdy stuff. For if life afloat was hard, life ashore was not much better— for the poor at any rate. On board ship, at least men's stomachs were full, and they knew exactly where their next meal was coming from.

The men lived and slept among the weapons and gear of the long decks. Their mess tables were fixed between the gun barrels and then hooked to beams when they were not in use. Every sailor had a knife which he carried about him, a spoon, an earthenware bowl, and a wooden plate. The ship's cook used a huge "copper" in his galley, which was forward, where he boiled the "salt junk." When he had fresh meat, it was roasted in great ovens. He burned wood, charcoal, and occasionally coal—whatever he could get.

The regular victuals included hard biscuit, which was often full of weevils, salt beef, salt pork, dried peas, oatmeal, coarse brown sugar, butter which was usually rancid, and cheese. The quality varied from fair, through bad, to shocking. But the rationing was strict, and few went hungry. In suitable countries fruit could sometimes be had, and oranges and lemons were much in demand. They helped prevent scurvy, the dreaded disease known to all seafaring men, which was the result of a deficiency of vitamin C. Occasionally sailors got food which even they could not digest, meat so tough, gristly, and fibrous that boxes could be carved from it which would take a high polish.

The fresh-water casks had to be carefully conserved and were replenished whenever possible. But there was never enough fresh water, and it often went bad. Salt water was used both for bathing and for swabbing the ship. Beer and rum generally took the place of drinking water: the beer was excellent and was a food in itself; the rum, which came from the West Indies, was fiery and tasted of molasses. Daily allowances of rum were liberal—half a pint mixed with a quart of water in the presence of the officer of the deck to make sure there was no cheating.

The British sailor may have lived a rough life, but he was generally cheerful. And in the crowded companionship of month after month at sea, there was far more kindliness than bullying. Without this quality, life would have been unbearable. Bullying existed, and it made trouble, but the

Portsmouth Harbor, on the southern coast of England, was the home base for Nelson's fleet. At right is the port as it looks today, with Nelson's ship, the Victory, *restored in drydock. Below is an engraving of Portsmouth as it was in Nelson's day.*

Purser

Sailor

Midshipman

Cook

ships that Nelson came to command were, without exception, happy ones.

A typical sailor of the fleet was a man of no education, narrow outlook, and cheerful disposition. Within his sharp limits, he was matchless. What he knew, he knew thoroughly, because his life depended on it. He could fight, sing, swear, grumble, and he knew how to jump to a word of command, on deck or aloft. By and large he was unbeatable, and he felt it. He thought of himself as being worth at least three foreigners. It is the only spirit in which to win battles, and that was his business.

It was precisely that readiness for combat that young Nelson had begun to doubt he possessed. Then, in the depths of his depression on board the *Dolphin*, and under the encouragement and kindly care of his captain, he began to reach some happier conclusions and to recover his health. He wrote later: "A sudden glow of patriotism was kindled within me . . . 'Well then,' I exclaimed, 'I will be a hero, and confiding in Providence, I will brave every danger!'"

Responsibility, promotion, war experience on land and water, were in fact all before him. The captain of the *Dolphin* had helped to bring back Nelson's self-confidence and inspire him with devotion to his navy. Nelson had found within himself the strength to meet a personal crisis more dangerous than his first taste of war at sea.

Thomas Rowlandson, the witty English caricaturist, painted a series of colorful seamen in 1799. Four of these are seen at left. The ship's crew was probably not so gentle in real life as the artist portrays the men here. Below, a merry group of sailors sings in the mess alongside a cannon. This etching was made by George Cruikshank, who was a popular Georgian satirist.

II

WAR IN THE AMERICAS

The pace of events quickened soon after Nelson's return to England. The American uprising, which Great Britain at first thought could easily be snuffed out, flared into a full-scale revolution. And it appeared that the French court, where Benjamin Franklin was exercising his effective brand of homey diplomacy, would soon intercede on the side of the Americans. Then Spain would follow, turning the Revolution into a global war.

Midshipmen of experience were in demand, and in September, 1776, Nelson was given the rank of acting lieutenant in H.M.S. *Worcester*. The *Worcester* was a ship of the line—which would correspond in relative size and function to a battleship in more recent times—the mighty backbone of the British Navy.

Nelson was just eighteen as he went on board the *Worcester*, saluted the quarter-deck, and met Captain Robinson. He was no longer uncertain of himself or his profession. All that stormy winter, as the *Worcester* crossed the Atlantic on wartime convoy duties, the young seaman served with diligence. In later years he wrote:

"Although my age might have been a sufficient cause for not entrusting me with the charge of a watch, yet Captain Robinson used to say he felt as easy when I was upon the deck as any officer in the ship."

In the spring of the following year Nelson faced another kind of personal ordeal: he was brought before a board of captains for the examination that would either confirm or deny him his lieutenant's rank.

One of the judges who gave Nelson his examination was his uncle, Maurice Suckling. Suckling, who as head of the Navy Board had great power, remained a faithful and

Spokesman for the American Revolution was Benjamin Franklin, here being hailed at the French court.

The earliest portrait of Nelson, by Rigaud, was begun in 1777. Fort San Juan, which the young captain seized from the Spanish, is in the background.

In this romantic painting, an unruffled Nelson departs from his ship during a gale to board a captured prize.

solicitous friend. Nelson had not expected to see him, and Suckling concealed their relationship. When the young man recovered from his first fluster, his answers were prompt and satisfactory. Everyone was pleased. Suckling then rose from his seat and introduced his nephew. The others showed surprise that in a navy where graft and favoritism were almost expected, Suckling had said nothing beforehand to indicate his interest. "No," he said, "I did not wish the younker to be favored. I felt convinced he would pass the examination well, and you see, gentlemen, I have not been disappointed!"

Suckling, who was then in charge of England's shipbuilding program, could ensure that the newly made lieutenant had a good ship and that he would be sent to an active area. Accordingly, Nelson was appointed to the frigate *Lowestoffe*. Her captain was William Locker, who had learned the art of war under the eye of a great leader, Admiral Lord Hawke. The ship's destination was the West Indies. Not only had Nelson been there before, but he knew that it was to be one of the decisive theaters of war. The West Indian sugar plantations were a great source of Britain's wealth.

The West Indies were indeed the richest trading area in the world at that time. They were also one of the main causes of the American Revolution and of Britain's war with France. American merchants had long been chafing under the British restrictions that limited the freedom with which they could trade among the Caribbean islands. Unless the Americans could persuade the French to help them, their lucrative traffic in rum, slaves, and molasses would be ruined.

Although Nelson's service in the *Lowestoffe* was his first experience of war conditions, he did not find life aboard the ship demanding enough to suit him. "Even a frigate," he wrote, "was not sufficiently active for my mind . . ." His zealous temperament and desire for action are illustrated by an event which occurred aboard the *Lowestoffe* while she was cruising out of Jamaica. In a style which may seem boastful, but which was plain fact, Nelson related the following incident:

"Whilst in this frigate, an event happened which presaged my character . . . Blowing a gale of wind, and a very heavy sea, the frigate captured an American letter of marque. The first lieutenant was ordered to board her, which he did not do, owing to the very heavy sea. On his return, the captain said, 'Have I no officer in the ship who

Above, a 1784 sketch by Cuthbert Collingwood shows Nelson with a wig. He lost his hair temporarily when ill with tropical fever.

can board the prize?' On which the master ran to the gang-way to get into the boat . . . I stopped him, saying, 'It is my turn now; and if I come back, it is yours.' This little incident,'' he continued, ''has often occurred to my mind; and I know it is my disposition that difficulties and dangers do but increase my desire of attempting them.''

Because of this kind of brash courage, Nelson was given command of the schooner *Little Lucy*, which acted as tender to the *Lowestoffe*. In this vessel, he made himself ''complete pilot for all the passages through the Islands situated on the north side Hispaniola [Haiti].'' He was then twenty, and it was while he was on the *Little Lucy* that he was to have one

Cuthbert Collingwood (in a later portrait at left) served with Nelson in the West Indies. There they formed a close friendship.

of those personal strokes of luck that could make a career in the navy of his time.

Admiral Sir Peter Parker arrived in the West Indies as commander in chief and at once took a fancy to Captain Locker's young pupil. He asked Nelson to transfer to his flagship, the *Bristol*, as third lieutenant, from which he quickly rose to be first lieutenant. Then he was given his next step, promotion to commander of the *Badger*. Parker wanted someone to take over this fast brig, and Nelson was picked. He was in charge of her only a few months. In June, 1779, his best friend, Cuthbert Collingwood, succeeded him, for that month Parker gave Nelson a

Nelson was sent to the West Indies to protect British trade from the Americans and the French. This 1750 French map shows the islands of the Antilles, right, where he spent much of his time. His major action occurred at Nicaragua, then known as Mosquitos Shore (below Golfe de Honduras, center).

further advancement. He was appointed to the frigate *Hinchingbrooke*, with the rank of post captain.

If the Admiralty confirmed the promotion (as in due time it did), Nelson would be set for life. Although still a few months short of twenty-one, he had reached a position in which he could command the largest of His Majesty's ships of war and from which he would, in the normal course of events, rise to the highest command. He was a young man who might go very far indeed. Nelson, in whom gratitude was strong, never forgot what he owed to his uncle for his start, to Locker for experience of war conditions afloat, and to Sir Peter Parker for quick advancement.

The year 1780 opened in the Caribbean with Britain's preparations to attack Spanish settlements in Nicaragua, Spain by then having joined with France and the American colonists against Great Britain. It was to be a combined land-and-sea operation, with the aim of capturing Fort San Juan, which was far up the river of that name, and

At left is a sketch of Fort San Juan, probably made by Nelson. In order to reach the fort, over which a huge British flag waves, Nelson's crew had to travel one hundred miles up the San Juan River, in the foreground. Inside the fort (at right) Nelson and his men attacked the Spaniards with swords and bayonets.

which was thought to be the gateway to rich inland cities.

Little sense was shown in planning or equipment. Soldiers and seamen toiled in heat and swamp, losing more men through disease than from the enemy. Nelson landed a large proportion of his ship's company, took part in every engagement, and earned himself the nickname of the Brigadier. "I quitted my ship," he wrote, "carried troops in boats one hundred miles up a river which none but Spaniards since the time of the buccaneers had ever ascended . . . I boarded, if I may be allowed the expression, an outpost of the enemy, situated on an island in the river; I made batteries, and afterwards fought them, and was a principal cause of our success." His words were confirmed in the report of the expedition written by the military commander, who said, in a generous phrase, that Nelson was "first on every service, whether by day or night."

But Nelson was not immune to the perils of the Central American climate, and once again, as in India, he came down with fever. He withdrew in a sloop to Jamaica, after having lost a large proportion of his men from sickness.

Among Nelson's earlier surviving letters is a sad note written from Lady Parker's house, where he went to recover. His hostess was away, and he was wretched. He wrote to a friend that the servants let him lie "as if a log, and take no notice."

However, relief was soon at hand, and once again it was a kindly fellow officer who helped him. William Cornwallis, a younger brother of Lord Cornwallis, the general who later surrendered to the victorious American forces at Yorktown, gave Nelson passage home in the *Lion*. He was a stout, ruddy man, some fourteen years older than Nelson; "[His] care and attention," said Nelson, "saved my life." Cornwallis proved to be another Captain Pigot, restoring health and confidence to the young and moody officer.

It was nearly a year before Captain Nelson was himself again. However, during that time he had not been too feeble to visit an artist, John Francis Rigaud, often enough so that a portrait could be finished. The picture had been started at the instance of Captain Locker before Nelson left home in 1777. This is a precious memorial, for it is the only surviving portrait which shows Nelson before wounds and suffering transformed him. Always aware of the value of what would now be called publicity, Nelson told Rigaud to include Fort San Juan in the background, with the British flag flying above it. Nelson had helped to capture the place, and he had actually sketched it with his own careful pen. If he lived to achieve nothing else, he hoped to go down in history as the young captain who had done so well in Nicaragua.

Three times, in later life, Nelson returned to the West Indies, but never with his early good fortune. In 1782, while commanding the frigate *Albemarle* in the final stages of the American Revolution, he made a disastrously unsuccessful attack on Turks Islands in the Bahamas, which were then held by the French.

The American Revolution had not been a good war for either Nelson or his navy, but he hoped to end up with a fine burst of personal glory. The French had occupied Turks Islands, and Nelson, who was serving in the area, thought that with his own ship and the help of one or two others whose captains were junior to him, he could turn the enemy out and plant the British flag.

He was wrong. The French were well prepared. They were in strong positions, and Nelson gave far too little

thought to the matter of how to get the better of them. He was beaten off with ease, and one of the officers whom he had induced to help him wrote home afterward to say that the whole business had been "undertaken by a young man merely from the hope of seeing his name in the papers; ill schemed at first, carried out without a plan afterward, attempted to be carried into execution rashly because without intelligence, and hastily abandoned at last for the same reason that it ought not to have been undertaken at all . . ."

These were harsh words to be written by one officer about another, but they were deserved. Nelson took them so much to heart that never again, in all his life, did he fail for the same reasons. Never again would he fail to plan, and he would always use his intelligence.

St. Eustatius in the Dutch West Indies offered a neutral harbor to rival merchantmen. Below are British, French, and Dutch ships.

Britain took the Caribbean island of Guadeloupe in 1759 and held it four years. Above, British ships in the harbor fire a salute, perhaps to the governor in residence. The French flag flies there today.

But Nelson's time in the *Albemarle* is also remembered because of a different view of him—this one seen through the royal eyes of Prince William Henry, the sailor son of George III, who was later to succeed to the throne as William IV. The Prince was then serving as a midshipman in the flagship of Lord Hood, and he gave the following account of his meeting with Nelson:

". . . [I] had the watch on deck when Captain Nelson of the *Albemarle* came in his barge alongside, who appeared to be the merest boy of a captain I ever beheld; and his dress was worthy of attention. He had on a full-laced uniform; his lank, unpowdered hair was tied in a stiff Hessian tail of an extraordinary length; the old-fashioned flaps of his waistcoat added to the general quaintness of his figure and produced an appearance which particularly attracted my notice; for I had never seen anything like it before, nor could I imagine who he was or what he came about. My doubts were, however, removed when Lord Hood introduced me to him. There was something irresistibly pleasing in his address and conversation; and an enthusiasm, when speaking on professional subjects, that showed he was no common being."

It was indeed becoming apparent to all who came in contact with Nelson that he was "no common being." One of the people to discern this was a certain Mrs. Frances Nisbet, the widowed niece of the president of the island of Nevis in the West Indies. While Nelson was serving his one and only peacetime commission in the Caribbean aboard the frigate *Boreas*, two years after the Turks Islands fiasco, he met and courted the charming and well-educated widow. She gave him friendship and love at a time when, despite his outstanding qualities, he had offended some of the islanders by his insistence that everything be done according to the letter of the British law.

Fanny Nisbet overlooked Nelson's officiousness; she saw only his energy and ambition. For his part, Nelson saw a young woman who was able to fill his social needs as well as those of his heart. He wrote her: "My love is founded on esteem, the only foundation that can make passion last." The couple were married on March 11, 1787, in the presence of Prince William Henry.

Soon thereafter the Nelsons—Captain Horatio, Fanny, and her son Josiah, offspring of her previous marriage—returned to England. It was peacetime, and there was little need for Nelson's services. He was paid off from the *Boreas* and languished in Norfolk on half pay. His only activity for the next five years was farming in the village of Burnham Thorpe, where his father was still the parson. He tried in vain to get a ship, but the Admiralty looked upon him coldly.

Then at last, in the year 1793, war reopened with France, which was then in the grip of a revolution which would change her form of government and which would reverberate throughout Europe. Experienced sea officers were once more in demand, and Nelson was given a ship of the line, H.M.S. *Agamemnon.* "After clouds comes sunshine," he wrote enthusiastically to his wife. At last he had achieved his wish, command of a big ship, and she was destined to serve in the Mediterranean with a fleet under Lord Hood, an admiral for whom Nelson had entire respect. His cup of happiness was full.

Nelson married the demure Frances Nisbet, above, at Nevis in 1787.

Nelson's friend Prince William Henry became King William IV.

III

THE AGAMEMNON

Nelson loved the *Agamemnon*, and he made his name in the fleet while he was her captain. The *Agamemnon* had been built twelve years before and had already seen battle under two admirals. She carried 64 guns, though the standard armament for a third-rate ship of the line like the *Agamemnon* was 74 guns. She had none of the great 32-pounders of the "74's" or of the three-decked ships of the first and second ratings, but she was well armed with 24-pounders on her lower deck and 12-pounders on the deck above. What Nelson valued particularly about her—apart from the fact that she was his—was that she could outsail most other battleships in Hood's fleet, and that she was both handy and well manned. She took her place in the line as would a modern battleship that had the speed of a cruiser.

She carried about six hundred officers and men, including a detachment of marines, and she could keep the sea for months on end. And unlike many of the ships that sailed with her, the *Agamemnon* was manned mostly by volunteers. The British Navy, despite the national emergency of the war with France, continued to have great difficulty finding crews other than pressed men and derelicts (the press gangs scoured the country for whatever material could be found). But Nelson, relying on the prestige of his family in the Norfolk area, had been able to attract a more willing breed. It was these men, who increasingly came to regard him as a leader worthy of love rather than fear, that Nelson intended to develop into his own kind of fighting force.

The *Agamemnon* could outrange or outsail anything she was likely to meet while on detached service. With her three stately masts, fore, main, and mizzen, crowded with canvas, her rigging and decks alive with men, she seemed to Nelson the finest thing afloat. Moreover, she was in a full sense his home. The officers were his friends. He had his wife's young son, Josiah Nisbet, with him as a midshipman. His great cabin, with its stern windows, was graced

On the long bowsprit of this storm-tossed third rate, seamen shorten sail.
Third rates were of a naval class designed to carry between 64 and 84 guns.

with his own belongings, and he was master in a world he knew and loved.

Nelson's politics were at best loyal and old-fashioned. He could not be expected to have any sympathy for the French revolutionaries who had executed their king and were bathing their land in blood. He believed in his king, and the idea of a government without a monarch to lend it authority repelled him. Nelson once counseled the son of a friend who had come to sea with him in these words: "There are three things, young gentleman, you are constantly to bear in mind: first, you must always implicitly obey orders without attempting to form any opinion of your own respecting their propriety; secondly, you must consider every man as your enemy who speaks ill of your king; and thirdly, you must hate a Frenchman as you do the Devil!"

It was with a mixed feeling of obedience and impatience, therefore, that Nelson accepted his orders: the

The British fleet abandoned Toulon in December, 1793. Above, Napoleon's troops storm into the city as monarchists clamber into the last boats.

A. J. Gros painted this study of Napoleon three years after Toulon.

Agamemnon would take up a station off the Mediterranean coast of France, watching and waiting to see what the French fleet would do. He would have preferred to have been on more active service than blockade duty; he could not have realized how vital such routine work would be to the twenty-year war that was now beginning. It would be responsible ultimately for the defeat of France.

As Nelson sailed into the Mediterranean and joined the rest of Admiral Hood's fleet off the port of Toulon in that August of 1793, he knew only that he would have to content himself with interrupting the enemy's shipping whenever he could; with watching the enemy in the harbor for any telltale signs of activity; and with pursuing whatever ships might slip out so doggedly that they could not escape. Such were the principles of an offensive blockade in the days of sail.

But on this one occasion the operations took an unusual form. For there was within Toulon a party that was loyal to the memory of the executed French monarch, Louis XVI, and that hoped to see his family, the Bourbons, restored to the throne. The group of monarchists were prepared to welcome Admiral Hood and his fleet—provided the Admiral could find troops to defend the city against the revolutionaries. Hood had under his command the sailors of his fleet, a number of British marines, and the men of the few ships which the Spanish king, a new and very temporary ally of Britain, had supplied. But he had no considerable land forces.

Nevertheless, Hood did occupy Toulon and immediately sent Nelson off to Naples, which was at that time an independent kingdom in the southern part of Italy, to ask for soldiers to help him garrison the port. The Admiral had reason to hope that his request would be granted, for King Ferdinand IV of Naples was married to the sister of Marie Antoinette, the imprisoned queen of France, and Ferdinand was full of zeal against the French Republic.

At Naples, Nelson found active friends. Foremost were the British minister and his wife, Sir William and Lady Hamilton. Sir William had been a soldier in his youth, and his thirty years at the Neapolitan court had not lessened his relish for a good fight. His wife, Emma, was a captivating beauty who shared her husband's fondness for things military. The sympathies of the Neapolitan prime minister, Sir John Acton, were entirely with Hood. In spite of his name and title, Sir John was Italian in speech and by adoption, having never lived outside Italy

TEXT CONTINUED ON PAGE 46

43

THE SHIPS
OF NELSON'S NAVY

In the foreground of this sketch, a single-deck frigate of 32 guns sails across the wind. She is steered by two seamen manning the large wheel from which cables lead to the rudder. Frigates were the "eyes of the fleet," sent ahead to scout out the enemy. Sailing with the wind toward the frigate is a two-masted schooner, a swift and lightly armed ship that was used for communications between the fleet and the home base. In the background is a ship of the line, which, like the Agamemnon, *had at least 50 guns and was used in the heaviest part of the fighting. She is "hove to," her sails so arranged that she drifts sideways down the wind, moving neither forward nor backward. A captain's gig, rowed by six sailors, moves among the ships.*

At Naples, Sir William Hamilton stands with King Ferdinand before a flaming torrent of lava from the volcano of Mount Vesuvius. Behind them are guards and the queen. At front left, the artist, Pietro Fabris, includes himself in the scene. This unusual watercolor is from Sir William's own volume on volcanos.

TEXT CONTINUED FROM PAGE 43

and France. As a statesman of honesty, he was invaluable in a court where that quality was rare.

Ferdinand and his court made much of the eager and newly arrived Captain Nelson. Dinners, receptions, and parades were held; better still, troops were promised. "You do business in my own way," Nelson said with admiration to Hamilton, while Emma touched him by her kindness to Josiah Nisbet.

The visit was cut short by news that a French corvette was at anchor off Sardinia, together with a small convoy from Turkey, bound for the port of Leghorn in northern Italy. Although, as his eye ranged the harbor of Naples, Nelson saw vessel after vessel, Neapolitan or Spanish, which could have gone in pursuit, he was assured that they

were one and all "otherwise employed." So for the honor of his country he himself set sail, at two hours' notice, and went out to seek the enemy.

He had no success: the corvette and her convoy had moved away into the unknown. Nelson had no orders to return to Naples, and it was five years before he was able to resume his lively friendship with the Hamiltons.

Hood's success at Toulon was short-lived, for he was forced to evacuate the city at the approach of revolutionary troops of the French Republic. Some four thousand Neapolitan soldiers had joined his forces, thanks to Nelson's efforts, but he still had too few men of quality to make the place secure. The French, on the other hand, were inspired in their attack by a young officer of artillery, Napoleon Bonaparte, to whom much of the credit for recapturing the town was due. This was the same Napoleon who was to rise to power in France and throughout all Europe until only England—and Nelson—opposed him.

The Neapolitan soldiers were routed. They were flung out of Toulon with the rest of the allied forces. The city was then given over to a massacre, such as so often adds horror to civil war. For the moment, the British had failed in this attempt to vary the pattern of blockade by more aggressive action. They had no choice but to return to the frustrating but effective work of blockading.

It was during the Toulon phase of the war that Nelson had his first taste of warfare at sea since the American Revolution. In October, 1793, while near Sardinia, he sighted a squadron of five French ships, all smaller than his own, but including three well-armed frigates. He had landed many men to serve ashore under Hood, and the *Agamemnon* was shorthanded. Nonetheless, Nelson went in pursuit of the enemy and engaged them for four hours. Then other French sails appeared on the horizon. Nelson, whose ship was beginning to be hit in her masts and rigging, wisely decided to break off the action.

After that perilous encounter, Nelson committed his thoughts to his private journal. They demonstrate that as well as the faith he put in his men and his ship, he had another sustaining faith which he had received from his father.

"When I lay me down to sleep I recommend myself to the care of Almighty God," he wrote, "when I awake I give myself up to His direction. Amidst all the evils that threaten me, I will look to Him for help, and question not but that He will either avert them or turn them to my advantage. Though I know neither the time nor the manner of my death, I am not at all solicitous about it because I am sure that He knows them both, and that He will not fail to support and comfort me."

If Admiral Hood's fleet was to be successful in its mission of blockading France's Mediterranean coast, another base was needed after the fall of Toulon. The Admiral's choice fell upon Corsica, that wild and lovely island between French and Italian waters. The fortified places on the island were in French hands, but many Corsicans had warm feelings toward England and were prepared to welcome a British rule. For many months during the winter of 1793 and the spring and summer of the following year, Nelson and his men were engaged in land-and-sea operations designed to secure the island. Nelson's picked band of seamen, nicknamed the Agamemnons, were tireless. They dragged guns up mountainsides, manned them, bombarded the enemy, and fought like first-rate soldiers. "My seamen are now what British seamen ought to be," wrote Nelson, "almost invincible: they really mind shot no more than peas."

From April to the end of May, 1794, Nelson served at the siege of Bastia on the eastern coast of the island; and

Below is the now tranquil harbor at Bastia, Corsica, which Nelson held after defeating the French. At Corsica, he was wounded by a splinter which brought about permanent blindness in his right eye.

FRENCH GOVERNMENT TOURIST OFFICE

after Bastia was captured, he was just as outstanding in the reduction of Calvi on the west. And it was at Calvi, when he was with the batteries on Corsica's mountainous shore, that Nelson received the first of his serious wounds. He had had minor setbacks before, of which he took no notice. "I am here the reed among the oaks," he had boasted. "All the prevailing disorders have attacked me, but I have not strength for them to fasten on. I bow before the storm, while the sturdy oak is laid low." On July 16, he wrote home:

". . . I was wounded in the head by stones from the merlon [parapet] of our battery. My right eye is cut entirely down; but the surgeons flatter me I shall not entirely lose sight of that eye. At present I can distinguish light from dark, but no object; it confined me one day when, thank God, I was enabled to attend to my duty. I feel the want of it; but such is the chance of war, it was within a hair's breadth of taking off my head."

What had happened was that the enemy, suddenly opening fire, had destroyed three British guns, and in the course of the bombardment Nelson was struck in the face by splinters, stones, and sand flung up by a shell. He bled profusely. Examination showed that he had received a deep cut which had penetrated the eyelid and eyeball. A few months later he wrote to his wife: "My eye is grown worse and is in almost total darkness and very painful at times; but never mind, I can see very well with the other."

Nelson's cheerfulness in the face of this grave injury, and his determination to carry on, were characteristic of him when he was in real distress. He would grumble ceaselessly at small matters but accept large misfortunes with stoic courage. For the remaining years of his life, Nelson had only one good eye, the left, over which he sometimes wore a green shade to help protect it from the southern glare. But he was not in any way disfigured, and his officers used to say that he saw better with one eye than most men did with two.

One of the purposes or hopes of the British activity in the Mediterranean was that the French fleet could be lured out of its safe harbors. And, at last in March, 1795, the French made a sortie in force from Toulon, with the idea of recapturing Corsica. Nelson was thereby given his first experience of a large-scale naval engagement.

Commanding the British Mediterranean fleet in that year was Admiral Hotham, who had replaced Hood. Admiral Hotham, learning of the sailing of the French ships, stood out to meet them. The ships maneuvered for some

This wooden figurehead from HMS Horatio, *built in 1807, shows Nelson with but one eye.*

time, inconclusively. Finally the French turned and ran, whereupon one of the largest ships, the *Ça Ira*, got into difficulty. Her mainmast and her fore-topmast were carried away by the wind and she was partially disabled. She was attacked at once by Captain Fremantle in the frigate *Inconstant* until he was driven off by two French ships of the line which turned up and took the *Ça Ira* in tow.

The *Agamemnon*, although one of the smallest ships of the line present, stood toward the French line of battle, and she gained so much on the rest of the fleet that she was soon on her own. For two and a half hours, bringing his broadsides to bear in turn, Nelson pounded away at his opponent—the *Ça Ira* losing over a hundred men, against seven wounded on the *Agamemnon*. Night then fell. But on the following day, March 14, the French ship was abandoned and the British colors were hoisted. One other vessel, the *Censeur*, was also taken.

Hotham thought he had gained a victory, since he had without doubt saved Corsica. "We must be contented," said the Admiral complacently. "We have done very well." Nelson disagreed.

"Now," wrote Nelson, "had we taken ten sail and allowed the eleventh to escape when it had been possible to get at her, I could never have called it well done. . . . Nothing can stop the courage of English seamen . . ."

Hotham was not a leader to Nelson's taste, though he liked the Admiral well enough personally. "I wish to be Admiral," Nelson confessed in a letter sent home to Fanny, "and in command of the English fleet. I should very soon either do much, or be ruined. My disposition cannot bear tame or slow measures. Sure I am, had I commanded our Fleet on the 14th, that either the whole French fleet would have graced my triumph, or I should have been in a confounded scrape."

Yet it was Admiral Hotham, not Nelson, who was fighting according to the best naval principles of the day. Most European military encounters of the eighteenth century were quite gentlemanly affairs. A battle was considered won not when the enemy had been annihilated but when the commander determined that he had received the greater share of honor. Hotham, therefore, was quite correct, by the thinking of his time, to be content with a limited victory.

For Nelson, victory had to be absolute, and he expected the rewards to be great. He loathed half measures, by land or sea. His new conception—which might be called total victory—was to revolutionize the warfare of his time. His method involved utter disregard for the conventional battle tactics. His approach could only be followed out with complete disdain for human life and personal safety.

Admiral Hotham had one more chance for a general engagement in the western Mediterranean, in July 1795. But again the affair was inconclusive, and again the *Agamemnon* did most of the fighting. Yet this time Nelson's services were properly recognized. The Admiralty showed him a singular mark of favor by appointing him a colonel in the marines. It was an honorary post, much coveted, which carried pay but no duties. Considering the land fighting which Nelson had experienced on both sides of the Atlantic, it was an appropriate distinction.

Nelson's next employment was in fact partly military. He was given command of a squadron detached from the main fleet. This squadron was ordered to cooperate with an Austrian army which was attempting, without much success, to stem a great advance made by the French into Italian territory. For many months his principal movements were around Genoa and Leghorn. Although he had some success in interrupting enemy supply ships, he had

A commodore's pennant flies from the topmast of the Agamemnon.

the disappointment of seeing complete failure on every side by the Austrian forces.

His greatest personal satisfactions were that Sir John Jervis had replaced Hotham as commander in chief, and that Jervis had ordered him to fly the broad pennant of a commodore. Alas, this could not be in the *Agamemnon*, for it had become necessary to send her home, since she was by now scarcely seaworthy. Nelson transferred to the *Captain*, a ship of 74 guns. As a commodore, Nelson held local rank senior to that of a captain. It was a useful way of giving an officer the status, though not the actual post, of a junior admiral.

The enemy grip on the shores of the Mediterranean was by now so extensive that it was clear the British fleet would soon be forced to leave the area. East of Gibraltar no British base was secure. The Spanish alliance had already crumbled, and for a time at least that country had joined hands with France. Nelson's role became defensive. Withdrawal was the order of the day, including the removal of garrisons even from Corsica. It is possible to imagine Nelson's bitterness when the order to evacuate Corsica—the island where he had lost his eye—was given by the Admiralty. The blockade for the time being was over.

Early in December, 1796, Jervis ordered Nelson to transfer to a frigate, *La Minerve*, and sail to Elba to take British troops and stores off that island, which is between Corsica and the Italian mainland. Soon after leaving Gibraltar, on December 19, Nelson encountered the *Sabina*, a Spanish ship of 40 guns. He attacked at once.

The battle raged for over two hours before the Spaniard, having lost two thirds of her men killed or wounded, struck her colors. She was commanded by Captain Don Jacobo Stuart, a descendant of the British royal house of Stuart. He was known to be one of the best officers in the Spanish service.

Nelson described the action to his brother William, saying that it opened with his "hailing the Don" and requiring immediate surrender. "This is a Spanish frigate," came the instant reply, "and you may begin as soon as you please!" Nelson added:

"I have no idea of a closer or sharper battle; the force to a gun the same, and nearly the same number of men; we having 250. I asked him several times to surrender during the action, but his answer was—'No Sir: not whilst I have the means of fighting left.' When only he himself of all the officers was left alive, he hailed and said he could fight

Sir William Hotham was Nelson's chief in the Mediterranean.

no more, and begged I would stop firing." Hardly had the guns ceased (and the boarding party been dispatched to the *Sabina*) than other Spanish ships were seen approaching. The next day Nelson was forced to abandon the prize, together with his boarding party, in order to look after his own ship. *La Minerve* was able to fight free of the enemy, but she could not prevent Spanish colors being rehoisted in the *Sabina*.

Soon afterward, prisoners were exchanged. Don Jacobo returned to Spain, while Lieutenant Thomas Masterman Hardy, who had commanded the prize crew, was able to rejoin Nelson. Hardy's return was an event far more significant than it seemed at the time. For Hardy was to serve

TEXT CONTINUED ON PAGE 56

Setting out to recapture Corsica, the French were met by Admiral Hotham's Mediterranean fleet. A beaten French ship, the Ça Ira (center), was pounded by Nelson's broadsides for more than two hours.

OVERLEAF: *Firing a final salvo, the British fleet sails off as the French forces occupy the port of Bastia in 1796. The Admiralty had ordered Nelson to evacuate Corsica.*

53

TEXT CONTINUED FROM PAGE 53

under Nelson's flag in all his great battles. He was to mature into Nelson's idea of the perfect executive officer, and it would be to Hardy that Nelson would one day tell his confidences and final hopes.

An incident that served to deepen the friendship between the two men occurred off Spain in 1797. Nelson had received orders to leave the Mediterranean; he was to sail with *La Minerve* to reinforce Admiral Jervis' fleet in the Atlantic. No sooner was the frigate clear of Gibraltar than she was sighted and pursued by two Spanish ships of the line. Colonel Drinkwater, an army friend of Nelson's who was taking passage with him, asked if there was likely to be an action.

"Very possibly," said Nelson, "but before the Dons get hold of that bit of bunting"—looking up at his commodore's pennant— "I will have a struggle with them, and sooner than give up the frigate I'll run her ashore."

Not long afterward, Nelson and his staff sat down to dinner. But hardly had the meal begun when it was interrupted by the cry, "Man overboard!" Hardy immediately

Thomas Hardy was Nelson's idea of the perfect executive officer. They became lifelong friends.

went off in the jolly boat to attempt rescue. But the sailor who had fallen overboard had been caught in a current which was flowing toward the pursuing Spaniards; he was never seen again. Presently, Hardy and the others in his boat were in difficulty. The current was strong, the Spaniards were catching up. The jolly boat seemed to make no headway back to the ship.

"At this crisis," so Drinkwater related, "Nelson, casting an anxious look at the hazardous situation of Hardy and his companions, exclaimed, 'By G——, I'll not lose Hardy. Back the mizzen topsail.'"

This order had the effect of checking the frigate's speed, and an encounter between unequal forces now seemed certain. But the watching Spaniards were surprised and confused by Nelson's action. The leading ship suddenly shortened sail, allowing *La Minerve* to drop down to the jolly boat and pick up Hardy and his men. By the time the enemy had recovered, the frigate was again under way. Soon she had lost sight of her pursuers. Nelson's cool courage alone had won his point. Hardy was safe.

When Nelson left the Mediterranean, his fleet passed the Rock of Gibraltar. Below, a French squadron sails past the giant rock, at the right, and into the Atlantic Ocean.

THE COMMODORE'S CHANCE

On the very day of his rescue of Hardy, Nelson had another adventure—one that was to begin the first great battle of his career. In the late evening, Nelson found himself sailing through a patch of fog. When it lifted, he could see that he was surrounded by an enemy squadron, although the fog still concealed him. Nelson kept close to the enemy long enough to note its strength, and then made his way to Jervis' rendezvous off Cape St. Vincent, Portugal, which he reached on February 13. He found the Commander in Chief expecting battle, and he was ordered to rejoin the *Captain*, the 74-gun ship of the line that was his command after the *Agamemnon*.

As Nelson had already discovered, the Spaniards were at sea in force. A fleet of twenty-seven ships had left Cartagena, the large Spanish port in the Mediterranean, for the Atlantic. They expected to be joined soon by a French squadron, and they also had to protect a convoy which included ships laden with mercury, a valuable cargo.

When Jervis sighted the Spaniards they were in no regular order: there was a strong force to windward of him under Admiral Córdoba, and another, more scattered, to leeward, making toward Cadiz. Jervis led his compact group of ships between the two enemy forces, meaning to keep them apart and then attack Admiral Córdoba. His plan succeeded, but he turned to make the assault somewhat late.

The *Captain*, flying Nelson's pennant, was the third from last ship in Jervis' line. Before Jervis had made his signal to "tack in succession," that is, to change direction, Nelson realized that the leading ships would not be able to catch up with Admiral Córdoba in time to prevent his joining the other group of Spanish ships. Nelson also realized that if he himself turned out of the line and made at once for a group of Spanish ships, he would be able to bring them under fire —and that was what he did.

The smoke of battle drifts across this column of British ships sailing between the two Spanish squadrons as action commences off Cape St. Vincent.

Such an act of initiative on the part of a subordinate was unparalleled in the history of the Georgian navy—and it has never been repeated. The line of battle was sacred. To leave it, without a direct order, meant court-martial and probable disgrace. Under a disciplinarian like Jervis, disobedience of any kind, however intelligent, demanded supreme courage, and it would need to be justified, up to the hilt, by success.

For a time the *Captain*, unsupported, sped toward a detachment of seven Spaniards, one of them Córdoba's own *Santissima Trinidad*, the largest fighting ship in the world. Nelson was soon joined by two old friends: in the *Culloden* came Troubridge, with whom he had served as a youth off the coast of India; in the *Excellent* came Collingwood, a companion of those days in the West Indies, who now commanded a ship with the best gun crew in the British fleet. Both ships were responding to new signals from Jervis.

The *Captain* came under heavy fire, suffering in sails and rigging. Her wheel was soon shot away, and seeing that she would be able to do no further service in the line that day, or even in a chase, Nelson ordered his captain, Miller, to close with the nearest Spanish ship. Then he called for boarders.

It was not the duty of a commodore to board and engage in hand-to-hand fighting—but Nelson was no ordinary commodore. What followed his assault on the Spanish *San Josef* needs telling in his own words:

Admiral Sir John Jervis

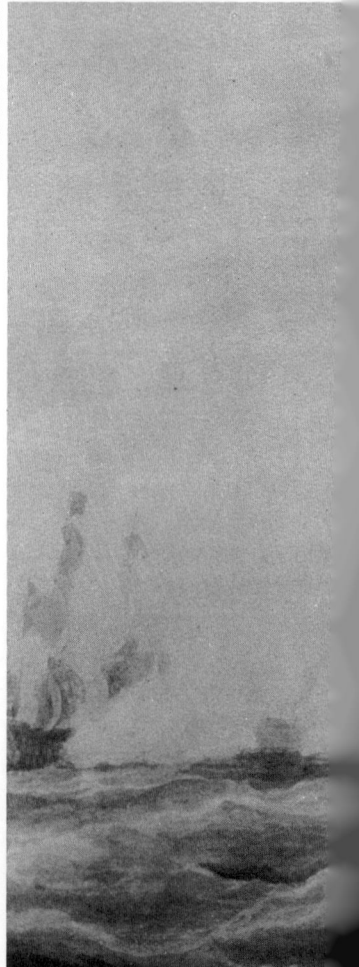

At right, Nelson in the Captain *engages the Spanish ships* San Josef *and* San Nicolas. *Above, he climbs aboard the* San Josef *to claim his prize.*

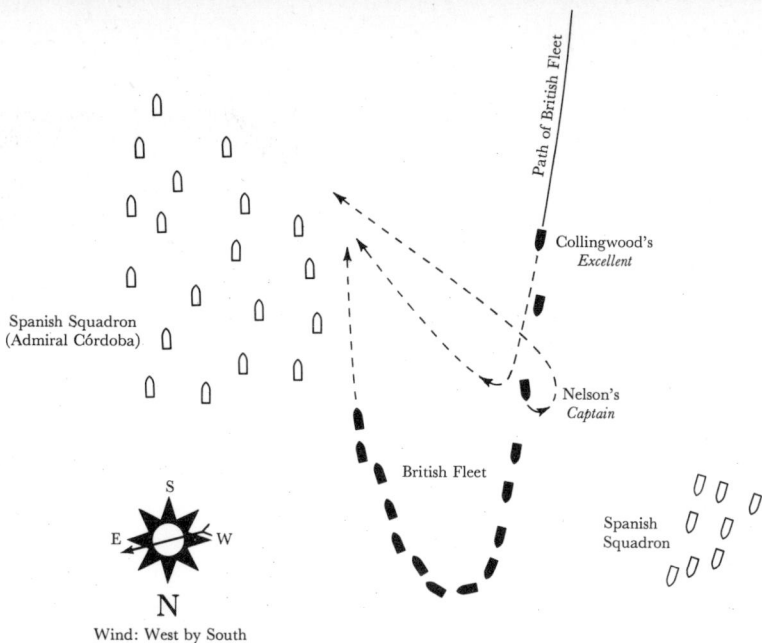

Spanish Squadron
(Admiral Córdoba)

Path of British Fleet

Collingwood's
Excellent

Nelson's
Captain

British Fleet

Spanish
Squadron

S
E   W
N

Wind: West by South

When the British fleet changed direction to attack the Spanish ships of Admiral Córdoba, its line resembled a shallow "V" (left). Fearing that the Spaniards would escape, Nelson swung across the top of the "V" and was soon followed by Collingwood in the Excellent.

Nelson stands on the quarter-deck of the San Josef *to receive the sword of
the defeated admiral. Amidst the debris of battle, Spanish officers and a
priest hold the dying man as Nelson's seamen, at right, arrive on board.*

"The first man who jumped into the enemy's mizzen-chains was Captain Berry, late my first lieutenant. He was supported from our spritsail yard . . . a soldier of the 69th Regiment, having broke the upper quarter-galley window, jumped in, followed by myself and others, as fast as possible. I found the cabin doors fastened, and the Spanish officers fired their pistols at us through the windows, but having broke open the doors, the soldiers fired, and the Spanish brigadier fell as retreating to the quarter-deck." A detachment of the 69th—now called the Welsh Regiment—was serving as marines and did splendidly throughout. Within a few moments the *San Josef* was in British hands. Just beyond her was an even larger ship, the *San Nicolas*, which had been run alongside her compatriot. Nelson ordered Captain Miller to send a party across the *San Josef* to take the other ship by storm. Nelson followed.

"When I got into the main chains," he said, "a Spanish officer came upon the quarter-deck rail, without arms, and said the ship had surrendered. From this welcome information it was not long before I was on the quarter-deck when the Spanish captain, with bended knee, presented me his sword and told me the admiral was dying with his wounds below . . . and on the quarter-deck of a Spanish first rate, extravagant as the story may seem, did I receive the swords of the vanquished Spaniards . . ."

The British took four Spanish ships on February 14. Two of them had surrendered to Nelson in person. It was thought at one time that the towering *Santissima Trinidad* had struck her colors, but she got away in the confusion and murk of the winter afternoon, though Admiral Córdoba had to shift his personal flag to a less damaged ship.

Having gambled, and having won his prizes, Nelson had now to face his admiral. He need not have worried. Before night fell, he went on board the *Victory*, from which Jervis exercised command, and was received with the greatest affection. The Admiral "used every kind expression," said Nelson, "which could not fail to make me happy." Jervis, soon to become Earl of St. Vincent in recognition of his triumph, knew a leader when he saw one.

Nelson had been bruised in the stomach during the fighting, and as the *Captain* was damaged, he moved to the *Irresistible*. This ship had a good surgeon, and, moreover, her condition was up to any assignment that might come along. Nelson stayed in her three months, during which time he made one foray into the Mediterranean to guard a final convoy withdrawing men and munitions from Cor-

TEXT CONTINUED ON PAGE 66

The sword above was given to Nelson by the dying Spanish admiral.
NORWICH GUILD HALL

63

Nelson fell from a bullet wound in the right arm while attacking Tenerife. Here his stepson, Josiah Nisbet, supports him and saves his life by stopping the bleeding. The bargeman behind has torn his shirt for a bandage.

64

*While Nelson recovered from the loss of his arm, this fashionable portrait
was done by Lemuel Abbott. Nelson wears the star of a Knight of the Bath;
at his neck is a medal awarded for service at the Battle of St. Vincent.*

65

sica and Elba. He was then given command of the inshore squadron off Cadiz, a Spanish port on the Atlantic side of Gibraltar. It was an active post for a very active man.

A few days after the Battle of Cape St. Vincent, Nelson became, by seniority, a rear admiral. "I never saw anything elevate [your] Father equal to this," wrote Fanny to her husband; but there was something even better in store. On Jervis' recommendation, Nelson was made a Knight of the Bath for his services in action. Henceforward, Rear Admiral Sir Horatio Nelson, K.B., would wear a star on his coat and would be seen for what he was, a man who had made his mark in the service of the country. He had no false modesty. He enjoyed success, recognition, and honor.

While Nelson was engaged in blockading the port of Cadiz with his inshore squadron, Jervis heard that a Spanish treasure ship had put in to the port of Santa Cruz in the Canary Islands, and he planned to capture her. Tenerife, the island concerned, was well defended, and the service would require an expedition. Nelson was chosen to lead it.

He was given four ships of the line, with his flag in the *Theseus*, together with three frigates and a cutter. He chose his own officers, who included Troubridge in the *Culloden* and Fremantle in the frigate *Seahorse*, successor of the ship of that name in which Nelson had had his brush with Hyder Ali. Fremantle actually had his bride on board.

Everything went wrong. Owing to unfavorable weather and currents, the landing boats were unable to reach the landing place on the island during the hours of darkness, and they lost all the element of surprise. The few parties able to get ashore were soon withdrawn, since they found the garrison alerted. Nelson then decided that he would lead a night attack in person. "Tomorrow," he wrote to St. Vincent on July 24, "my head will probably be covered with laurel or cypress"—laurel for a conqueror, cypress for mourning.

Josiah Nisbet pleaded to go with his stepfather. "No," said Nelson. "Should we both fall, what would become of your poor mother!" "I will go with you tonight," said the youth, "if I never go again." Nelson let him have his way.

It was well that he did so, for Nelson's boat was heavily fired upon as she neared the shore. Just as he was about to land, a shot shattered his right arm. Nisbet, who was near, saw that Nelson could not stand, and heard him exclaim: "I am a dead man!" The youngster placed him in the bottom of the boat, then took a silk handkerchief from his neck, and with the help of one of the bargemen, bound the silk

Nelson had this coat of arms designed when he became a Knight of the Bath, after Cape St. Vincent. On the left, a sailor trampling on a Spanish flag holds a staff which carries a broad pennant. At right, the British lion tears the Spanish flag. On top of the crest is the San Josef. The motto is "Faith and Works." The crest itself had always been in Nelson's family.

tightly round and above the injured limb, staunching the flow of blood. The boat then withdrew into the darkness, picking up survivors from the cutter *Fox* as she made her way back to the squadron.

It was the *Seahorse* that Nisbet first sighted, but nothing would induce Nelson to board her, even at risk to his life, for he needed immediate care. "I would rather suffer death," he said, "than alarm Mrs. Fremantle by her seeing me in this state, and when I can give her no tidings of her husband."

When the *Theseus* was found, Nelson refused help in getting aboard. "Let me alone," he said. "I have yet my legs left, and one arm. Tell the surgeon to make haste and get his instruments. I know I must lose my right arm, so the sooner it is off the better."

The amputation was performed in the early hours of the morning of July 25, and it was successful. Next day, so the surgeon noted, Nelson "rested pretty well and quite easy. Tea, soup, and sago. Lemonade and tamarind drink."

The "rest" was relative. The expedition was in ruins, and although Troubridge got a party ashore, he could do little. His ammunition was soaked, his men were outnumbered, and there was nothing for it but retreat.

The Spaniards, traditionally courteous, were ready to parley. They behaved, said Troubridge, "in the handsom-

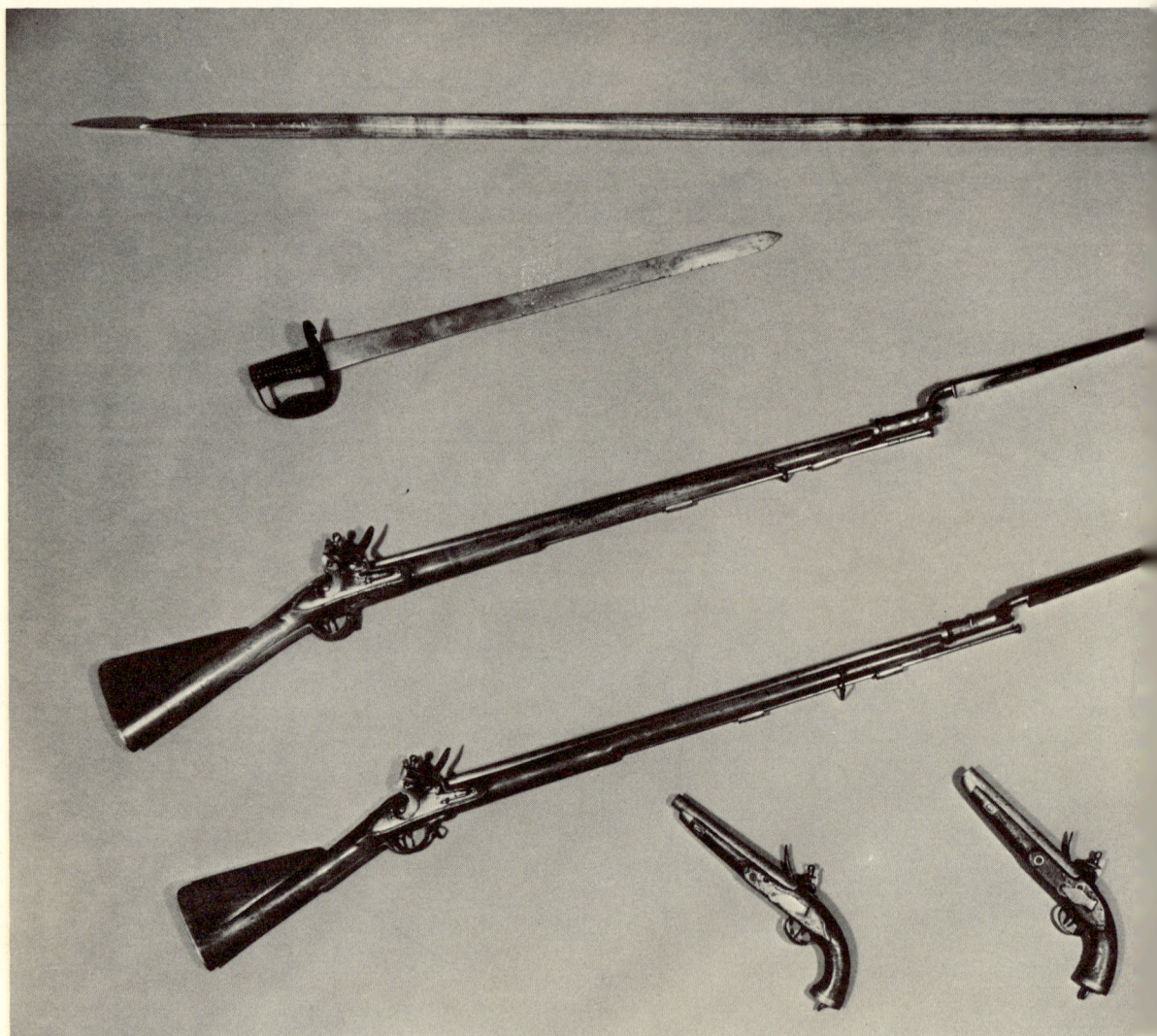

The weapons shown above were used when seamen fought hand to hand. At top is a boarding pike. Other arms are cutlasses, muskets with bayonets fixed, and pistols.

est manner, sending a large proportion of wine, bread, etc., to refresh the people, and showed every mark of attention." They even lent boats so that the British could withdraw in comfort. Nelson, not to be outdone in politeness, begged the Spanish governor's acceptance of a cask of English beer and a large cheese.

It was just as well Nelson did not board the *Seahorse*, for when Fremantle did return to his wife, he also was wounded, and his injury, though slighter, was as troublesome as Nelson's, and needed constant attention. By an odd chance, he too had been hit in the right arm while landing.

On August 16 the squadron rejoined Lord St. Vincent. Nelson had written from sea, slowly and with his left hand,

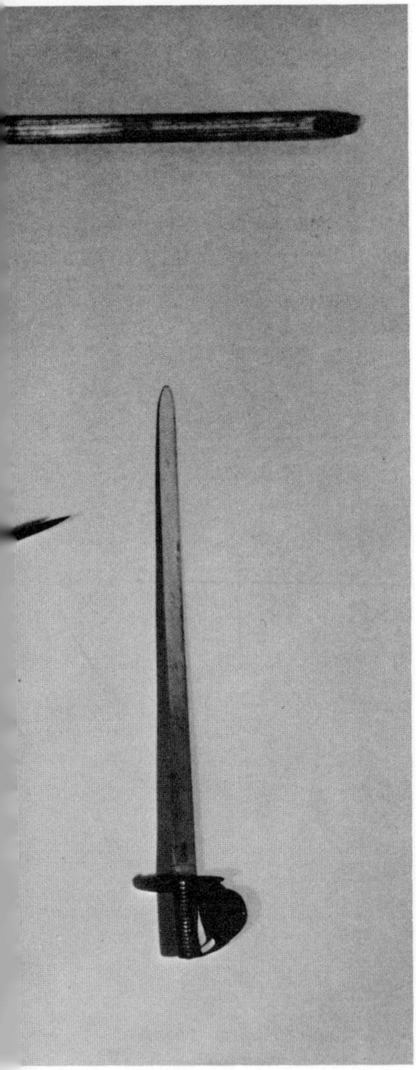

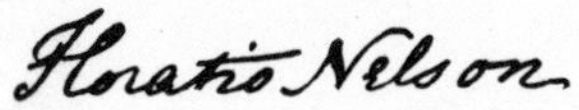

Horatio Nelson

As a lieutenant in the West Indies

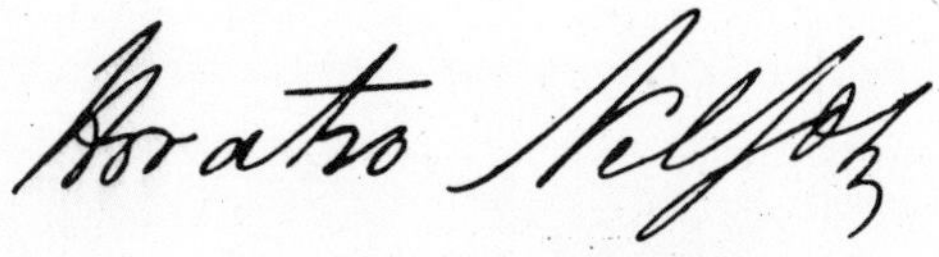

Horatio Nelson

Before he lost his right arm

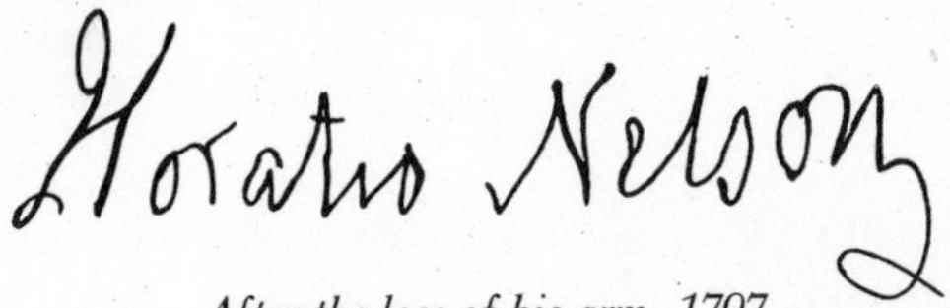

Horatio Nelson

After the loss of his arm, 1797

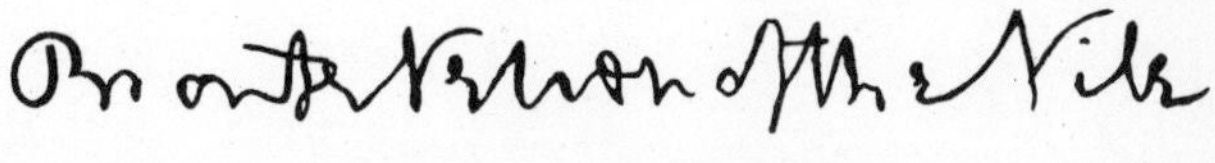

Bronte Nelson of the Nile

After the Battle of the Nile

Nelson & Bronte

In the last years of his life

Nelson's signature (seen in the samples above) changed considerably—from the small, neat script of his youth to the bold scrawl he executed later when he was given the added title of Duke of Bronte.

to say that "a left-handed admiral will never again be considered useful . . . the sooner I get to a very humble cottage the better, and make room for a better man to serve . . ."

Less accurate words were never written. Nelson indeed went home in the *Seahorse* with the Fremantles, and with the *Theseus'* surgeon, Dr. Eshelby, to look after him; and he recovered before Fremantle.

When Nelson joined his wife and his father in England after more than four years' absence, it was with all the eager, affectionate zest they had known of old. It was a hero who returned, renowned and decorated. He brought Fanny news that young Josiah's conduct at Tenerife had won him an early promotion.

THE MEDITERRANEAN

Nelson could now consider himself the complete sea officer. He had served east and west, in frigates and big ships, in failure and success, by land and sea. The fortunes of his country were for the moment at a low ebb, but they were soon to mend.

On land the revolutionary French armies were everywhere victorious, and Napoleon was making a name which would ring throughout the world. But at sea Britain flourished, even though she fought alone and for the time was denied the Mediterranean. Lord St. Vincent, with Nelson's inspired help, had shown that the old-style sea battles, formal and indecisive, could be transformed into raging melees, with victory going to the boldest. Henceforward, Nelson's purpose would be to train his captains, to infect them with his own fiery spirit. He would take them to the enemy, and in battle itself would lead them to victory.

He was in England for seven months recovering from the loss of his arm. At first his stump pained him continually, but at last in December he was able to compose a note to the rector of the church where he worshiped. It said simply: "An officer desires to return thanks to Almighty God for his perfect recovery from a severe wound, and also for the many mercies bestowed upon him." By the early months of the year 1798 the doctors declared that Nelson was well enough for active service, if he wished to have an appointment.

The Admiralty was eager to employ him. There were many rumors of what Napoleon would do next. One consistent report was that the French general would lead an invasion of England; in February, 1798, Napoleon made a visit to the French and the Flemish channel ports to survey the project. But that desperate bid for world mastery was not to be attempted so soon. Napoleon concluded that the French Navy was not yet ready for the assault.

Another rumor was that the French were preparing an

Nelson's fleet rests in the calm harbor of Naples in June, 1798, two months before the Battle of the Nile. Mount Vesuvius looms in the background.

Before invading Egypt, Napoleon captured Malta. Here he has left his flag-ship to accept the surrender of the island. Pictured at right is the ill-fated Admiral de Brueys, appointed by Napoleon to command the invasion squad-ron. Like Napoleon himself, he is shown with his hand thrust inside his coat.

expedition to the East, and that Napoleon would command it himself. On May 17 a French corvette was captured, and the British were able to confirm the fact that a vast armada was being fitted out in Toulon. If Egypt was the object of Napoleon's expedition, one of the vital links in England's trade empire was at stake. It became imperative for the British fleet to re-enter the Mediterranean and find out what was afoot.

To his great pleasure Nelson was sent in the flagship *Vanguard* to serve with Lord St. Vincent. "The arrival of Admiral Nelson has given me new life," said the Commander in Chief. Within a few days the eager but still very junior Admiral had been given the task he would have chosen above all others. It was he who was to find and shadow Napoleon's fleet.

At first, everything went against him. The *Vanguard* was dismasted in heavy weather and was only saved from running ashore by the help of Captain Ball of the *Alexander*. Nelson's frigates became separated and returned to Gibraltar. But presently he was reinforced by some of Lord St. Vincent's best ships, bringing his force up to fourteen ships of the line. Yet his squadron had a major limitation: there was only one vessel that could be used for scouting,

and that was the brig *Mutine*, now commanded by Hardy.

And Nelson's greatest need was for news. He could learn nothing. The French had sailed—but where to? Sicily? Malta? Egypt? Nelson sent Captain Troubridge to Naples, hoping his friends the Hamiltons—that well-informed minister, Sir William, and Emma, his ever-active wife—could help him. But it was all in vain. The French had vanished. Then Nelson learned that Napoleon had taken the island of Malta, left a garrison there, and sailed away, presumably to Sicily. But Nelson was convinced that the French were sailing to Egypt. After anxious consultation with his captains, he decided to carry the search to Alexandria, far to the east. When he reached the city, he found the port deserted, and no sign of Napoleon. Utterly dejected, Nelson beat his way back to Sicily.

However, he had been right when he guessed that the French were making straight for Egypt. In fact, on his way to Alexandria, Nelson had overtaken Napoleon's expedition. One night Nelson had been so close that officers in the French flagship had heard the British signal guns. But the British squadron had never sighted the French fleet. What had happened was that Nelson's pursuit had been too swift; he had arrived in Alexandria ahead of Napoleon.

In Sicily, where he was watering and provisioning his ships, Nelson received news that Napoleon's fleet had been seen steering to the southeast about four weeks earlier. Once again Nelson consulted his captains, and deciding he had been right after all, he sailed a second time for the land of the pharaohs.

By this time the French army was ashore in Egypt. Having eluded Nelson and the rest of the British Navy, Napoleon went on to one of his greatest conquests. He seized Alexandria and prepared to march southeast to Cairo, the ancient capital from which the Turkish overlords ruled Egypt with England's blessing.

But Alexandria did not offer a safe harbor for the fighting ships of Napoleon's fleet. De Brueys, the French admiral, anchored them therefore in Aboukir Bay, not far from the Rosetta, or western mouth of the Nile River. It was there, on the afternoon of August 1, 1798, that Nelson's long search ended: the masthead lookout called out that the enemy had been sighted.

Every one of the British captains knew his duty. For during the weeks of the vain pursuit between Sicily and Egypt, Nelson had consulted with them often, had coached them on what should be done when the French were found,

TEXT CONTINUED ON PAGE 78

The Swiftsure's chaplain drew this map of the Mediterranean, tracing Nelson's search for de Brueys. Eluding Nelson, the French anchored in Aboukir Bay, below.

75

As the sun sets, Arabs on shore excitedly watch the fast-developing action between the two powerful fleet

he first ships of Nelson's squadron (in the background) are beginning to round the head of the French column.

TEXT CONTINUED FROM PAGE 74

had made them into a "Band of Brothers." He had used that term himself, taking the phrase from Shakespeare's *Henry V.*

When the French were discovered, it was comparatively late in the day, but no one doubted that Nelson would attack at once. Signals were brief: "Prepare for battle"; then another to indicate that Nelson would concentrate on the enemy's front and center. By Nelson's general plan, overwhelming force was to be brought against part of the enemy line. Ships were to anchor by the stern, with ropes attached to their anchor cables to keep them at the right angle for firing most effectively. And having blasted one of the enemy's ships from that position, they would, if need be, raise their stern anchors and move down the line to the next sitting duck.

Four lights were to be shown at their mizzenmasts to identify them as British ships, so there should be no confusion when daylight was gone. Captains were to keep measuring the water's depth as they entered the bay so that ships did not ground on the shoals.

As the British line gradually took shape, with the certainty of a mighty battle, Nelson, who had been on edge for weeks, suddenly grew cheerful, ordering dinner to be served there and then. Such was the pace of the days of sail that even with the enemy in sight a fighting man could fill his belly before he set to work.

Whether de Brueys' thoughts were confident, as Nelson approached, will never be known; for he did not survive to say. But he had had every chance to take up the strongest position possible. His squadron, thirteen ships of the line including the huge flagship *L'Orient*, was anchored in a curve running from northwest to southwest. Behind his squadron were four frigates, and behind the frigates were shoals and the sandy shore. Near the front of the French line was a small island where de Brueys had placed a few guns. On the face of it, the anchored ships looked impregnable. The squadron presented a packed range of batteries comparable to a mighty fort, which no one but a madman —or a genius—could attack without extreme risk of disaster. Parties of French were ashore getting fresh water, but de Brueys had them recalled in case the man who was approaching should attempt the seemingly impossible. De Brueys was ready. He might even have smiled at the thought that he had provided against every likely hazard.

At 5:40 P.M. Nelson, unperturbed, signaled for close action. Shortly before 6:30 Captain Foley of the *Goli-*

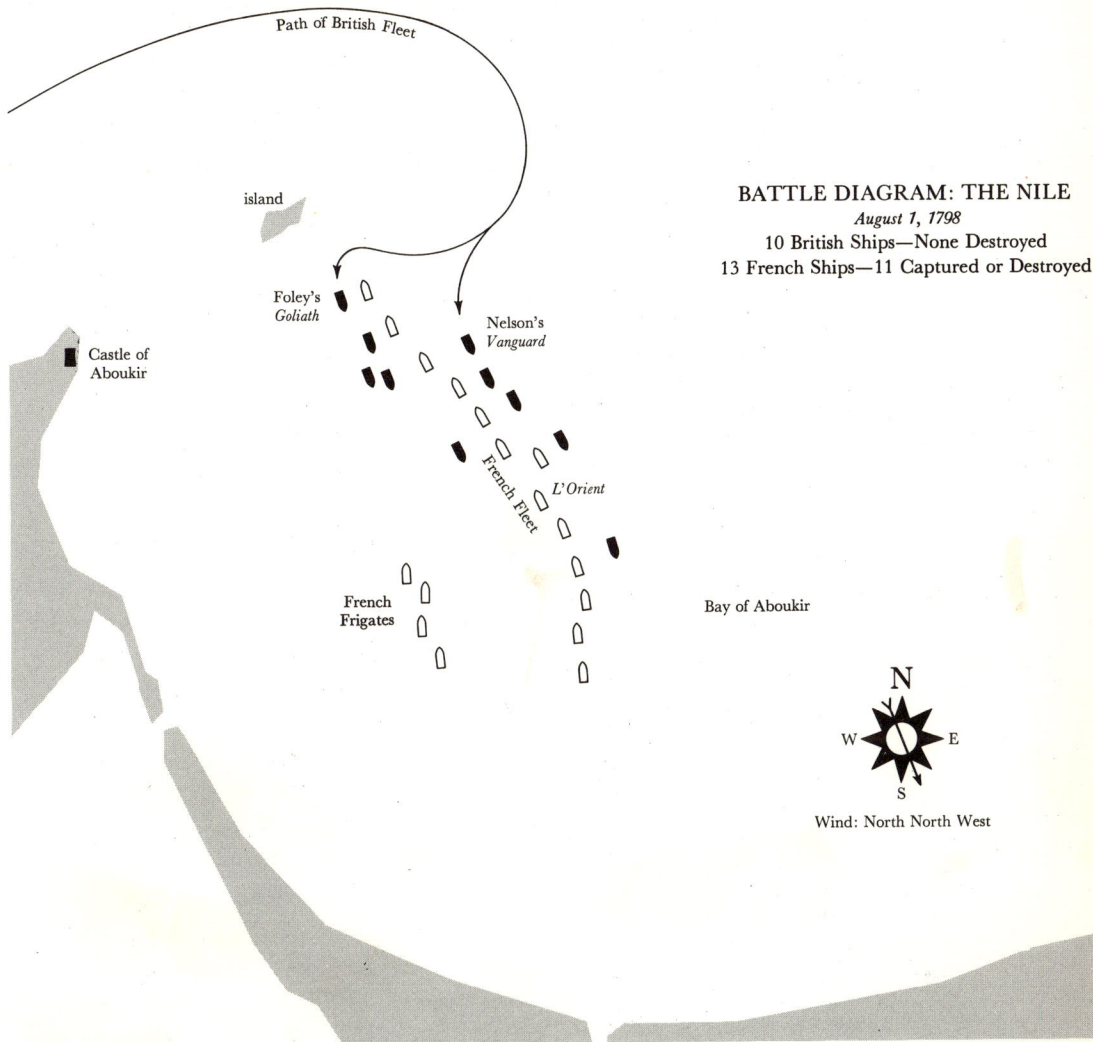

Path of British *Fleet*

island

BATTLE DIAGRAM: THE NILE
August 1, 1798
10 British Ships—None Destroyed
13 French Ships—11 Captured or Destroyed

Foley's
Goliath

Nelson's
Vanguard

Castle of
Aboukir

French Fleet

L'Orient

French
Frigates

Bay of Aboukir

N
W   E
S

Wind: North North West

Without orders, but inspired by Nelson's example at Cape St. Vincent, Captain Foley sailed around the head of de Brueys' anchored fleet. Nelson took the second half of the British line down the outside of the French ships, none of which could come to the other's aid.

ath, who was leading the British ships into the bay, had one of those flashes of insight that can mean the difference between victory and repulse. His duty was to attack the first ship, *Le Guerrier*, and from the seaward side; but as details of the scene grew clearer, as he drew closer under heavy fire, he saw all of a sudden that there would be room to pass round the head of the leading enemy ship and attack her from inshore. Her captain would not have reckoned on such an act: her landward-pointing guns might not be ready—and so it proved. *Le Guerrier* became an easy prey, and Foley's bold course was followed by Hood in the *Zealous*, Gould in the *Audacious*, Miller in the *Theseus*, and Sir James Saumarez, Nelson's second-in-command, in the *Orion*.

The French line was by then well and truly outflanked.

The leading ships could be attacked on two sides. Part of de Brueys' force could be crushed before the rest could help. In fact, his ships had not been anchored close enough to one another; nor had de Brueys mounted enough guns on the island to thwart Foley's plan. The battle itself was half won before it had really begun.

Nelson's *Vanguard* was the first ship to attack the French from the seaward side, and this for a good reason. By the time he had brought her broadside to bear, the evening had become too dark to repeat any such maneuver as Foley had achieved. Any of the later ships would have been foolish to attempt it. These ships, *Defence, Minotaur, Bellerophon, Majestic, Swiftsure, Alexander,* and *Leander,* would follow Nelson in succession, each one finding an opponent. Only the *Culloden,* with Troubridge in command, came to

During the battle, in the cockpit of the Vanguard, *Nelson (above) is treated for a head wound. At the left a seaman writhes in pain as the doctor prepares to amputate his leg. Nelson was not seriously hurt, and later he was taken on deck (right) to watch the explosion of the French ship* L'Orient.

grief by running ashore on the tip of the sandy island. The incident drove Troubridge half crazy, but at least he was able to save others from sharing his fate by serving as a beacon to the vessels coming behind him. Thirteen British were opposed to an equal number of the enemy, but the weight in guns was heavily in favor of the French.

Action continued far into the hours of darkness, and the few who slept that night did so from exhaustion, beside their guns. One after another the French hauled down their colors or cut their anchor cables and ran the ships aground.

The most spectacular moment occurred about ten o'clock, when the French flagship, *L'Orient*, was seen to be on fire. Much of the damage had been done by the *Bellerophon*, though she herself, outgunned, had been driven into the night with her masts crippled and most of her officers

The doomed L'Orient, *de Brueys' massive flagship, explodes at the height of the Battle of the Nile. When she first caught fire, British ships downwind from her withdrew, fearing the effects of the coming blast. But the* Alexander *hung on (above), pummeling her huge opponent until the very end.*

killed or wounded. Then the little *Leander*, the *Alexander*, and others had taken up the work until it was clear beyond doubt that *L'Orient* was doomed. After blazing for some time, she suddenly blew up, with a noise which could be heard by French troops in Alexandria, thirteen miles away. Most of her company, de Brueys included, perished with her, and also lost was an immense treasure, much of it seized by Napoleon from the Knights of Malta.

One of the youngest persons present, Theophilus Lee, a midshipman in the *Swiftsure* (he was not yet eleven but had already served at the Battle of Cape St. Vincent), saw the episode from start to finish. He heard from survivors how de Brueys, having lost both his legs, was seated, with tourniquets on the stumps, in an armchair facing his enemies; he was giving directions for putting out the fire when a cannon ball from the *Swiftsure* put an end to his life.

Nelson himself, like his French opponent, had come under heavy fire and had been wounded at almost the same time. He had been hit in the head by a piece of iron shot. Blood streamed down across his good eye at such a rate that he thought it must be the end. He was led below where the surgeon was tending others, but at the whisper of the Admiral's approach, Doctor Jefferson broke away to see to him. "No," said Nelson, "I will wait my turn with my brave fellows." It was the kind of consideration sailors never forget. Struck on the head, and completely blinded by the blood, Nelson was sure death was near. He called for the chaplain, and saw to it that messages were given for Lady Nelson. Then he sent for Captain Louis of the *Minotaur* to thank him for the noble support his vessel had given to the flagship.

In fact, Nelson's wound was messy but not dangerous. The surgeon stitched it up, and soon he was able to return to the upper deck where he could see the last moments of *L'Orient*. He ordered the *Vanguard*'s only undamaged boat to pick up some of *L'Orient*'s crew he could see struggling in the water. Then, before the battle was over, he sent for his secretary so that he could begin dictating a dispatch. The man was in no state to write, nor was the chaplain, so Nelson himself, with guns thundering around him and the night bright with explosions, penned these words to Lord St. Vincent: "My Lord, Almighty God has blessed His Majesty's Arms in the late Battle by a great Victory over the Fleet of the Enemy . . ."

When morning broke, it was upon devastation unique in the annals of sea warfare. "Victory is not a name strong

TEXT CONTINUED ON PAGE 87

Aboard the Vanguard, *Nelson (top right) cele-brates the British victory. One man in the group of sailors at the center plays a fiddle while a Turk (bottom left) smokes a long pipe.*

The HERO of the NILE.

Nelson was proclaimed a hero when the news of his victory at the Nile reached England. In the cartoon at right, he is bedecked with colorful trappings: he has on a peer's robe, the jewel and star of a Knight of the Bath, and on his hat he wears a diamond aigrette. Below, model ships in London's Hyde Park re-enact the famous battle scene fifteen years later: the "French" are anchored in the foreground.

86

enough for such a scene," said Nelson. Of the thirteen French ships of the line and the four frigates which had opposed him, all but four were either smoking hulks, sunk, held as prizes, or helplessly grounded. Of the four ships which escaped, two were mere frigates. The survivors were led away by Admiral Villeneuve, unpursued, since no British ship was in a condition to chase them. Napoleon called Villeneuve lucky. The French admiral did not share his opinion.

The Battle of the Nile was not merely a triumph for Nelson and his squadron, it was of world consequence. It was the first large-scale reverse suffered by the French since the war opened, and it meant the ruin of their Egyptian expedition. Napoleon could, and did, go on to conquer Egypt, but as he had lost his fleet, his army could never return home except by English permission. And although Napoleon himself contrived to escape from Egypt in a fast vessel, that was the most he could hope for personally.

News took far longer to travel then than now, and the *Leander*, which carried Nelson's dispatches, was intercepted off Crete by *Le Généreux*, one of Villeneuve's surviving ships; but Nelson had sent duplicate dispatches to Naples in the *Mutine*. When the victory was announced throughout Europe, every country but France rang with jubilation. The unbelievable had happened. Napoleon was not invincible. There was still hope for Europe while the British Navy could produce a Nelson.

When the news reached the Hamiltons in Naples, Emma fainted from excitement. She was not alone. Even the grave Earl Spencer, head of the Admiralty, fell flat outside his office in London when the dispatch at last reached him, so great had been his anxiety. For Napoleon's expedition had threatened British interests far beyond the Mediterranean; the whole East had been at stake.

One of Nelson's first actions after the engagement had been to send an officer overland to spread the news throughout Asia, for his early voyages and experiences had helped him to think in terms of world strategy. Every letter home on public matters had long shown that he saw the war as a whole, not merely locally. Young as he might be—and he was still short of forty—he found himself, through his own efforts, in a position to influence events in every continent.

His personal prestige was as remarkable as his victory. And it was his sure conviction that the God in whom he trusted had led and preserved him. Nothing astonished the French prisoners more than the thanksgiving services held

Nelson's victories were often commemorated in folk art. Above is an enamel box showing the L'Orient *in flames.*

in every British ship after the action. In the French Navy, worship of God had been abolished along with the ancient monarchy.

King George III made Nelson a peer; he was thenceforth to be called Lord Nelson of the Nile and Burnham Thorpe. He received tribute from every quarter. But by the time the honors began to flow in upon him like a golden flood, he was far from the scene of his triumph. Sending Sir James Saumarez to Gibraltar with the prizes, he himself sailed in the *Vanguard* to Naples.

Nelson, like his battered ship, needed care and attention. He still had a painful head concussion. Although his wound soon healed, it left a scar which he tried to cover with a lock of his hair, which was by now sandy-gray. He had recurrent fever, and it was the thought of the kindness and ability of the Hamiltons which led him to seek their help. At Naples, his ships could repair. And there he could depend on the experience of Sir William Hamilton, who was the senior British overseas emissary in the Mediterra-

Pictured above are Queen Mari Carolina and, right, King Ferdinan

88

nean area, to relieve him of a great burden of diplomatic correspondence. There he could recuperate. There, in a friendly city, he could contrive new ways of pressing on with the war.

One of the results of the victory at the Nile was that it stimulated the king of Naples, Ferdinand IV, into action against the French. His wife, Maria Carolina, needed no urging, for she could never forget that her sister, Marie Antoinette, had died on the guillotine as queen of France. On Nelson's advice Ferdinand sent an army north to attack the French who were then occupying Rome. It was bad advice, and it led to disaster. After some temporary allied successes, the French gathered strength, and the Neapolitans were hurled back. Following up their advantage, the French army invaded Naples, and Nelson soon had the sad task of conveying the royal family, the Hamiltons, and a flourishing British colony to the safety of Sicily. In August, Nelson had been a conqueror. By Christmas, he and his friends were in exile. Malta was still under French occupation. The French army was advancing in Egypt and Syria, and it seemed, for the time at least, as if a great victory had led to a sad reverse.

Nelson spent weary months at Palermo, comforted by the Hamiltons, managing his scattered fleet, and recovering his health. Then slowly matters began to improve. The French made themselves detested at Naples, and at last, in the summer of 1799, Nelson was able to restore Ferdinand to his mainland dominions. This was achieved through the bravery of an army of Neapolitan partisans supported and sustained by British sea power. Yet it was not a happy return, for it was accompanied by acts of vengeance and tyranny.

The Neapolitan king had many defects, but ingratitude was not one of them. He made Nelson a Sicilian duke, giving him a large estate at Bronte—and he loaded him with gifts. But because of his two-year stay at a foreign court, Nelson had vexed the home authorities, and even Sir William Hamilton fell into disfavor.

The distinguished diplomat was now close upon seventy. His major passion had been the antiquities of Italy; his disappointment at being called home to England was understandable. In the last year of the eighteenth century, a broken man, he had his final glimpse of his beloved Bay of Naples.

Also understandable was the attitude of Lady Hamilton. Some thirty years younger than her husband, she was nat-

A Neapolitan traitor was hanged from the yardarm of a ship in Nelson's squadron. At left, the dead man floats in the water while King Ferdinand and Sir William Hamilton lean over the deck's rail. Nelson and Emma Hamilton are at the right.

of Naples. The royal couple gave these miniatures to Lady Hamilton.

urally attracted to the vibrant young naval hero who begged her hospitality. In 1800 she and her husband and Nelson made a triumphant tour of Austria and Germany on their way home to England. She and Nelson were always together, everywhere cheered and feted.

A description of a gala evening in Vienna during their journey was written by an old friend of Nelson's, Lady Minto. She wrote that he appeared "a gig, from ribands, orders, and stars." But, she continued, "He is just the same with us as ever. I don't think him altered in the least. He has the same shock of hair and the same honest, simple manners. . . . He is devoted to Emma, he thinks her quite an angel, and talks of her as such to her face and behind her back, and she leads him about like a keeper with a bear. She must sit by him at dinner to cut his meat, and he carries her pocket handkerchief."

And it was Lady Hamilton, rather than Lady Nelson, who received the first cheers with him upon landing in England. The crowds in the harbor city of Yarmouth dragged Nelson's carriage through the streets, and when he and Lady Hamilton appeared later on the balcony of their hotel, they were hurrahed even more lustily than they had been on the continent. Lady Hamilton wore a flowing dress decorated with oak leaves and acorns, with coronets, anchors, and oval garlands enclosing the words "Nelson and Bronte."

Lady Nelson had been instructed to go to London and await the official reception there. When she and Lady Hamilton finally met in the capital the next day, they must have recognized each other as rivals at first glance. Two more different women would be hard to imagine. Fanny Nelson was virtuous, socially impeccable, colorless; Emma Hamilton was coarse, uninhibited, brilliantly colorful. It could not have been long before Lady Nelson saw that her worst fears had been realized. Nelson and Lady Hamilton had become lovers; the marriage was in ruins.

Yet Lady Nelson had her own kind of courage. And although it might have been possible for her to go on with the pretense that the much-honored Nelson was still hers, she did not. In the spring of 1801, after some months of trying to put the best face on things, she determined to leave. They were separated, and their house was sold. In an age of great men and tumultuous events, she was a slight woman who maintained her dignity.

George Romney painted a youthful Emma Hamilton as a Greek goddess (left).

Lady Nelson was about forty when this portrait was painted in 1797.

Sir William, age sixty-four in this picture dated 1794, died in 1803.

VI COPENHAGEN AND

Nelson had not been many months at home before he was ordered into the Baltic Sea. The Admiralty was eager to avoid the possibility of scandal over Lady Hamilton. They also wanted to give Nelson the chance of further fighting. The Baltic was not a part of the world he would have chosen, a cold area in a cold season; but sea officers went where they were ordered, and Nelson's new duty was both difficult and important. He was appointed second-in-command of an expedition led by Sir Hyde Parker. The objective was to prevent the fleets of Denmark, Sweden, and Russia (and the valuable supplies which were drawn from those countries) from being used in the service of France. By this time Napoleon had made his country master of Europe, and if Britain was to fight on, as she intended, it must be with her fleet unthreatened by the Northern Powers.

The fact that Nelson was not made commander in chief was in itself a form of reprimand. The Admiralty considered that he had taken too much upon himself at Naples, and they may have been right. They intended to teach him a lesson in humility.

They chose the wrong man. Nelson had a way of saying "I will be first"—and it was not an idle boast. Parker, a rich man, newly married to a young wife, was no fit choice for a task which required the utmost resolution. Nelson—and the Admiralty—had to use the spur before he would give the order for the fleet to set sail.

Parker failed at first to trust Nelson with his confidence. And Nelson replied by doubting Parker's courage and wisdom. It seemed to Nelson that the whole expedition, which would concentrate initially on bringing Denmark into line with Britain's concept of neutrality, was doomed to failure if Parker's timid and unwarlike course were followed. Nelson heard that the plan was to send a polite diplomat ahead of the fleet; the diplomat would present an ultimatum saying that Denmark should cease cooperating with

Nelson's division leads the British fleet to the attack on Copenhagen. As the ships sail through the Sound, they pass Cronenburg Castle at Elsinore.

BOULOGNE

Nelson fought at Copenhagen to prevent the Baltic powers from serving France. Paul I of Russia (above) was an ally of Denmark and Sweden.

France—and Admiral Parker was all too willing to wait peacefully offshore for the diplomat's return. Nelson's reaction to this procedure is recorded.

"All I have gathered of our first plans I disapprove most exceedingly; honor may arise from them, good cannot. I hear we are likely to anchor outside Cronenburg Castle, instead of Copenhagen, which would give weight to our negotiations. A Danish minister would think twice before he would put his name to war with England, when the next moment he would probably see his master's fleet in flames, and his capital in ruins."

By March 19, 1801, the English fleet had reached the Skaw, the northernmost tip of Denmark, whence the broad channel of the Kattegat extends southward, between Sweden and Denmark, until it reaches the island of Zealand, on whose eastern side lies Copenhagen. On the 23rd, news reached Parker that the British ultimatum had been rejected, and that Copenhagen was preparing to be attacked. Parker then asked Nelson to come on board his ship. "Now we are sure of fighting I am sent for," Nelson noted. "When it was a joke I was kept in the background." He disliked councils, though he had sometimes used them. "If a man consults whether he is to fight, when he has the power in his own hands," he wrote later, "*it is certain that his opinion is against fighting.*" Experience made him italicize the words. After the council, which was inconclusive, Nelson wrote a considered letter to Parker which summed up his thoughts in a way that finally persuaded the reluctant commander.

". . . the more I have reflected," he said, "the more I am confirmed in opinion that not a moment should be lost in attacking the enemy. They will every day and hour be stronger; we shall never be so good a match for them as at this moment. . . . here you are, with almost the safety, certainly the honor, of England more entrusted to you than ever yet fell to any British officer."

Nelson then dwelt on the various ways by which Copenhagen could be approached, and ended with sentiments first uttered by the great Earl of Chatham which he loved to quote: ". . . I am of the opinion the boldest measures are the safest; and our country demands a most vigorous exertion of her force, directed with judgment."

It was decided that Nelson should lead the attack in person, while Parker would provide a covering force that would lie off the city. The Danish fleet, supported by land guns and by the Trekroner batteries, had been drawn up at anchor in a line in front of the city. The Danish captains had had time to prepare: their base was immediately behind them, and they could await aggressive moves by the English with confidence.

Nelson was given ten ships of the line—slightly more than he had asked for—together with frigates, sloops, and smaller vessels. His idea was that when the wind favored him, he would move close in. And if his bombardment proved effective, it should, if necessary, be followed by a landing.

There were good omens. The first was that Nelson would fly his flag in the *Elephant*, and his captain would be Foley, the man who had seized his brilliant moment at Aboukir. Another was that when the fleet had passed Cronenburg, where there was danger from both Swedes and Danes, the Swedish guns never opened fire, and the Danes wasted their ammunition, firing often but hitting nothing.

TEXT CONTINUED ON PAGE 98

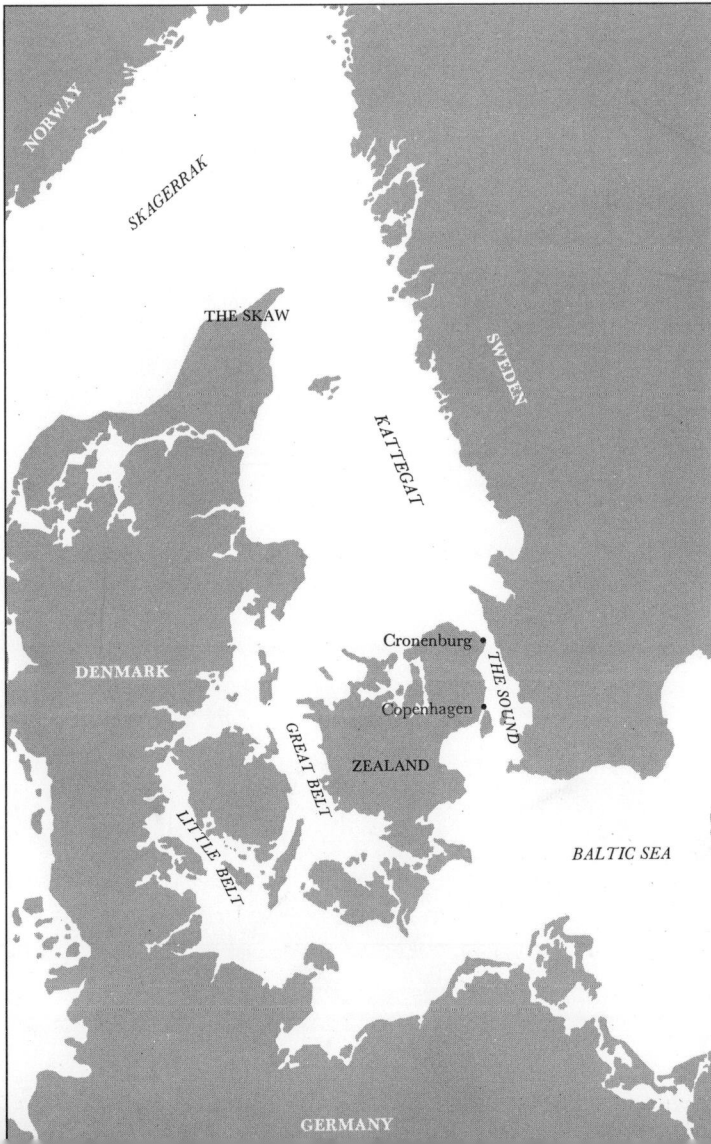

To reach Copenhagen, Nelson went around the Skaw (top center) and through the Kattegat to the Sound.

Entering Copenhagen Harbor, three British ships ran onto the shoals (foreground). The others, with Nelson

ip sixth in line, ran the gantlet of enemy fire. At right is a reserve squadron of British artillery vessels.

TEXT CONTINUED FROM PAGE 95

During the dark hours of April 1, with Hardy and other chosen officers, Nelson was able to reconnoiter the Danish line. "It looks formidable to those who are children at war," he wrote, "but to my judgment, with ten sail of the line I think I can annihilate them."

Opposite Copenhagen lay a shoal called the Middle Ground. On its eastern side was a passage called the Outer Deep; on its western side was Kings Channel where the Danish fleet stood. Nelson had to take his vessels south through the Outer Deep, anchor at the southern end of the Middle Ground, then wait for the wind to change so he could sail north into Kings Channel and bring his broadsides in succession against the eighteen anchored Danes. Once committed, there could be a stunning victory or utter defeat—precisely the battle terms that Nelson always desired. There could be no retreat, for at the northern end of the Danish line were the Trekroner batteries, and no ship was likely to survive their devastating fire.

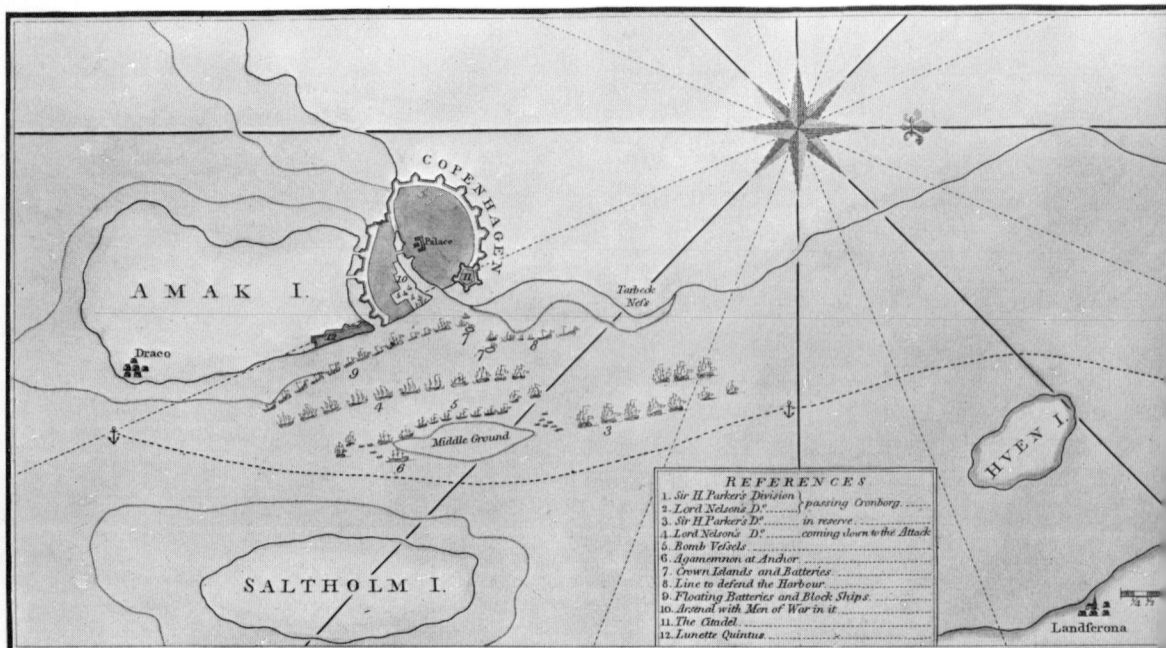

This English chart, published immediately after the Battle of Copenhagen, shows the passage of the British fleet through the Sound, past "Cronborg" Castle (1 and 2), to the first anchorage off Copenhagen. While Sir Hyde Parker's covering squadron lay off the capital (3), Nelson proceeded to the second anchorage beyond the Middle Ground and thence to the attack (4). His ships had to sail between the Danish ships and floating batteries (5 and 9), and toward the Trekroner batteries (7) and the city's massive citadel (11).

Nelson spent the rest of the night dictating his battle orders so they would be ready for his captains the moment he had a favorable wind. Reports kept coming in that the wind was indeed changing. By daylight on April 2 it was right for an attack.

As at the Nile, ships were ordered to anchor by the stern. They were to proceed down the Danish line after each opponent had been silenced. But in the confusion of the day, the careful plans became disorganized. The pilots who were to guide the ships around the shoal showed hesitation, and during the course of taking up their stations, three ships (the *Bellona*, the *Russell*, and Nelson's beloved old *Agamemnon*) went aground and could take little part in the battle. Thereafter it was sheer slogging under the worst conditions of early nineteenth-century warfare; as the fire opened and became heavier, all the advantages —the number of cannon, the superiority of position—were definitely with the Danes.

After several hours of bloody fighting, during the course of which Sir Hyde Parker suffered painful anxiety since his larger ships could take no part owing to their deep keels, he gave the signal to discontinue action. "The fire is too hot for Nelson to oppose," said Parker. "A retreat must be made. It would be cowardly in me to leave Nelson to bear the whole share of the failure, if failure it should be deemed."

The result of Parker's action was unexpected. Colonel Stewart, who was serving in command of a detachment of soldiers in Nelson's flagship, recorded it as follows after the signal lieutenant had reported Parker's message:

"He [Nelson] continued his walk, and did not appear to take notice of it. The lieutenant, meeting his Lordship at the next turn, asked whether he should repeat it. Lord Nelson answered, 'No, acknowledge it.' On the officer returning to the poop, his Lordship called after him. 'Is [my] No. 16, for close action, still hoisted?' The lieutenant answering in the affirmative, Lord Nelson said, 'Mind you keep it so.' He now walked the deck considerably agitated, which was always known by his moving the stump of his right arm. After a turn or two he said to me, in a quick manner, 'Do you know what's shown on board of the Commander in Chief? No. 39!' On asking him what that meant, he answered, 'Why, to leave off action. Leave off action!' he repeated, and then added, with a shrug, 'Now damn me if I do!' He also observed, I believe to Captain Foley, 'You know, Foley, I have only one eye—I have a right to be

blind sometimes'; and then with an archness peculiar to his character, putting his glass to his blind eye, he exclaimed, 'I really do not see the signal!'"

Parker's act cost at least one gallant life. Captain Riou, who had already proved himself an officer to Nelson's liking, was engaging the Trekroner with his frigate; he turned away in obedience to Parker's signal No. 39, saying, "What will Nelson think of us?" That instant he was killed by a shot. Nelson's judgment that it was to be victory or ruination that day was confirmed.

And his defiant confidence was justified. The retreat signal had hardly been flown before the Danish fire at last began to slacken, and Nelson sent ashore a flag of truce with a message (carefully sealed so that it should not appear to have been written in haste) in the following terms:

TO THE BROTHERS OF ENGLISHMEN, THE DANES
Lord Nelson has directions to spare Denmark, when no longer resisting; but if the firing is continued on the part of Denmark, Lord Nelson will be obliged to set on fire all the floating-batteries he has taken, without having the power of saving the brave Danes who have defended them.

These were bold words for the commander of a battered fleet in danger of its life; but their boldness was convincing. Firing immediately ceased, and Nelson was able to arrange an armistice with the prince regent of Denmark, who had been ashore near the line of battle, cheering his people on.

The battle had been a close contest, and Nelson considered it his tactical masterpiece. Ships were then believed to be no match for shore batteries, and the Danes had, in effect, turned their fleet into a series of forts. British casualties had been heavy, nearly a thousand killed and wounded, and over three times that number of Danes had suffered in defense of their capital. Nelson had been able to capitalize on what his fire power had won by seizing the right moment for his aggressive note.

His activity did not cease when the shooting stopped. Parker allowed Nelson to conduct all the negotiations with the Danish prince which followed immediately upon the action. "The more I see of his Lordship," wrote Captain Hardy, "the more I admire his great character, for I think on this occasion his political management was if possible greater than his bravery."

Nelson was able to secure the terms he wanted—that Britain should have unimpeded entry into the Baltic, and that the Danes should not place their fleet at the service

As Parker signaled retreat, Nelson raised a telescope to his blind eye. Here he tells Foley he cannot see, and a sailor beside him smirks.

As Danish fire slackened, Nelson, above, prepared his message to the Danish prince. It was then carried ashore with a flag of truce.

of France. But before the treaty could be implemented, news came of the assassination of the czar of Russia, Paul I, and of the accession of Alexander, whose intentions, it was believed, were more likely to be friendly toward Great Britain. Perhaps all of the blood that was shed at Copenhagen had been in vain.

Soon after the Battle of Copenhagen, Sir Hyde Parker was recalled, and Nelson succeeded to the post of commander in chief. It was one to which he had proved his right in no uncertain way, not only because he had triumphed but because victory had been won under the most difficult and delicate conditions he would ever face.

As he had expected after having been so long in Italian sunshine, the Baltic made Nelson ill. He asked to be recalled as soon as matters were settled, for the time at least, with the Northern Powers. The Admiralty met his wishes, but after a brief holiday with Sir William and Lady Hamilton, he was given a new and arduous responsibility.

Napoleon had massed a great army on the northern coast of France, and threatened Britain with invasion.

The threat was almost as old as the war itself, but French training had been intensified, and landing vessels of every kind were being collected in increasing numbers. Napoleon declared that if he had command of the Channel for twenty-four hours, England would be doomed.

It was the business of the British fleet never to allow control of the Channel to pass into enemy hands. Yet the big ships could not be everywhere at once, and they needed support from flotillas of small craft. These were numerous but untrained, and Nelson's mission was to put new life into the defense. It was uncongenial work for an admiral who had made his name as a fleet tactician, but, as was his way, he threw himself into the task with all his vigor.

Napoleon planned to invade England; and the designer of this fan-shaped print had some novel ideas of how to do it. He showed the English fleet being burned by fire and projectiles from balloons and a floating tower.

A young officer who was serving on his staff described him as being here, there, and everywhere. Nelson was characteristically engaged in keeping people alert, the Admiralty included.

"We got down to Sheerness," the officer wrote on one occasion, "and were received by the acclamations of the people, who looked with wild but most affectionate amazement at him who was once more going to step forward in defense of his country. He is the cleverest and quickest man, and the most zealous in the world. In the short time we were at Sheerness, he regulated and gave orders for thirty ships under his command, made everyone pleased, filled them with emulation, and set them on the qui vive . . ."

The plan above shows the start of Nelson's hit-and-run assault on the French flotilla moored outside Boulogne. The British left their ships at anchor (top) and boarded small boats in which they attacked the French line along the shore.

Nelson "made everyone pleased"; that was his secret. Everyone felt his quick, imaginative sympathy. Morever, he believed, as always, in what he called a "home stroke" against the French mainland. His business was to defend his native shores—but, like Sir Francis Drake before him, he believed that the best defense was attack. He had not been many weeks in his new command before he was planning an assault on Boulogne, the center of French preparations. Although he would take no part in the action as a fighting man, his orders were typical of his whole attitude in war.

"When any boats have taken one vessel, the business is not to be considered as finished," he wrote, ". . . a sufficient number being left to guard the prize, the others are

immediately to pursue the object by proceeding to the next, and so on until the whole of the flotilla be either taken or totally annihilated, for there must not be the slightest cessation until their destruction is completely finished."

The attack was made on August 15, 1801, but the French were fully prepared, and it was repulsed with heavy British losses. Nelson lost one of his favorite officers, Captain Edward Parker, and he was convinced that all would have been well if he had led the assault in person.

It mattered little, for within a few weeks a temporary peace was signed between Great Britain and France. Thus both Copenhagen and Boulogne, where Nelson had been called upon to fight bloody battles in tight quarters far from the open sea, might be considered fruitless actions. But Nelson recognized that if England was not ready to demonstrate her willingness to fight mercilessly on any and all occasions, the war, and the world, would be lost.

The treaty enabled Nelson to enjoy the longest spell ashore he had been allowed since the war opened. He seized the chance eagerly. He had acquired a property at Merton in Surry which he shared with the Hamiltons, and for more than a year he savored the pleasures of the country in whose cause he had faced so many dangers.

VII

THE VICTORY

In the words of Lord St. Vincent, supreme command in the Mediterranean was a post for "an officer of splendor." It was to that station, when hostilities with France were resumed in 1803, that Nelson was sent again. His flag was flown in the *Victory*, a ship which had borne St. Vincent in his triumph six years earlier. The underlying reason for the new outbreak of the war was that Napoleon's quest for complete control of Europe had not ceased. It would not cease until the French emperor was finally defeated on the field of Waterloo many years later. But the immediate excuse for the new hostilities was that the French could not tolerate the continuing British occupation of Malta.

The English intended to keep possession of Malta as one of the few bases left to them in the Mediterranean. They were determined not to let control of that sea, or any other, pass into French hands. For British sea power was the one barrier which stood between Napoleon and world mastery.

Napoleon still dreamed that he could short-cut his way to victory by a quick and successful invasion of England. His armies, refreshed and ready, were again gathering near Boulogne. And at that moment the English government in London seemed almost committed to assisting his plan of breaking through the defensive cordon of British ships. With singular lack of wisdom, the government had let the navy fall far below strength. Nelson might fly his flag in the *Victory*, but for the watch upon France's southern coast, which he was ordered to maintain, he could at first depend on only a handful of ships, some of them nearly worn out. Never was resolute skill in making the best of slender means more urgently needed.

Nelson in uniform was rarely without his medals (above). Seen in the shadow of the Victory *at left are four awards he wore on his chest: beneath the star of a Knight of the Bath are a Sicilian, a Turkish, and a German order.*

In calling once more upon Nelson, the Admiralty judged soundly. His experience had by now made him soberly responsible, and there were no two opinions about his genius as a fighting leader, least of all among the enemy. The *Victory*, his new home, was perhaps the finest first rate ever built. She had been afloat since Nelson was in his cradle, but she had recently undergone a large repair which was practically a rebuilding; moreover, she was capable of a surprising turn of speed. Nelson came to love her as he had once loved the *Agamemnon*, and for his flag captain he had the incomparable Hardy.

As commander in chief, with interest covering a wide area, Nelson was given an appropriate retinue. It included two secretaries, one for foreign and one for home correspondence. There was Captain Murray, a capable and seasoned chief of staff, and the surgeon and the chaplain. Always sociable, Nelson kept a hospitable table, at which officers from ships in his fleet were welcome. To minister to his needs he had a trained domestic staff whose head was Chevalier, his steward.

The ship herself was over 200 feet long, with a beam of 52 feet. Her mainmast, with its topmast and topgallant, rose 175 feet above the deck. She was "tall" indeed, and with her immense spread of sail, she was one of the most complex and lovely creations of man's hand. She carried

Merton Place, above, became Nelson's home when he returned to England in late 1801. At right some furniture from his cabin is arranged before a window at the Victory Museum, Portsmouth. The Victory *is in the distance.*

The ornate stern of the Victory, *above, remains the same today as in Nelson's time. Some other details of the restored flagship have been slightly altered (note the glass in the gun ports). The lower gun deck is pictured at right.*

104 guns. She had a complement of over eight hundred officers and men and was so self-contained that many of her people (Nelson included) did not set foot ashore for many years at a stretch. This was a feat of endurance made possible by the harmony that prevailed on board. Without exception, Nelson's ships were "happy" ones. There was little sickness and no discontent. Those who did not fit were sent home. Those who manned the great sea castle that dominated the Mediterranean knew that nothing afloat could match her in good order and weight of metal.

The captain's quarters, immediately beneath the poop at the stern of the ship, included a day cabin, a dining cabin, and sleeping quarters. Nelson's accommodations, on the deck below, were even more spacious. His dining cabin took up most of the width of the ship, and he had his own cooking arrangements. The ship's company, who lived forward, relied for their heated meals upon a huge iron stove, with chain-turned spits for roasting, and ovens for baking the "duff" (a flour pudding) the sailors loved. The galley chimney emerged through the upper deck, not far from the ship's bell, which was struck every half hour to mark the time of day. Below Nelson's range of cabins were the wardroom and the smaller cabins of subordinate officers. Deeper in the ship were stores, cables, ammunition, and huge casks of fresh water.

From Nelson's quarters, with their spacious outlook from the stern galleries, their fine furnishings, and their portraits of Emma Hamilton, orders went forth daily.

Nelson soon established his method of operation. His

TEXT CONTINUED ON PAGE 114

PHOTO PRECISION LTD.

THE VICTORY: A SAILING FORTRESS

For all the Victory's great size and capacity, not a corner was wasted, as this cutaway drawing of the 200-foot ship shows. Below the upper deck were three gun decks, on which a six-foot man could not stand without stooping. Nelson's day cabin (1) and night quarters (2) were on the first of these; the galley (3) on the second. Running up through the decks were

the masts and the deep ship's pumps (4). Below the waterline were vast holds for storing food (5), shot and powder (6 and 7), and sails (8). Power for the ship was supplied by the towering network of spars and sails, but the ship's heavy ropes were man-hauled by capstans (9). To supplement the cannon, sharpshooters were stationed high above the deck in the "tops" (10).

TEXT CONTINUED FROM PAGE 111

was to be a distant watch, not a close blockade, for his tactic was to draw the enemy out, not to keep him in, since the French could only be destroyed on the open sea. Nelson stationed frigates inshore, but he himself stood away with his larger ships, hoping to tempt an adventure. He depended upon Sardinia for supplies, and his main anchorage was near the island of Maddalena, off the extreme northeast coast of Sardinia.

The months of waiting were rarely enlivened by French sorties. Not once, in the years 1803 and 1804, was there a chance for more than a skirmish. The French, as soon as they learned of Nelson's strength and whereabouts, withdrew quickly to their base at Toulon. Nelson had ample time to ponder the circumstances of the war in which he was engaged, and to consider the nature of his opponent. He could also define his wishes for the navy to which he had dedicated his life.

A Frenchman, so he concluded, would always be a land animal; but if he wished to extend his conquests, he would one day have to face Britain squarely on her own element— the sea. As for the war, Nelson could see no end to it. Yet he knew that if ever he himself had the chance of another large-scale clash with a French fleet, then, if he were successful in his aim, that fleet would no longer exist. And in that case, however many years the war might last, France could never win sway over the world. She might hold what she had gained, if the subject peoples would let her, but she could do no more.

As for the Royal Navy, Nelson had shown that given imaginative leadership, there was scarcely a limit to what the British sailor could do. Nelson had brought heroism into the line of duty. He had shown how enterprise could help victory and how the formal rules of old-style warfare could be disregarded. He had demonstrated that a melee could be brought about in which, so he believed, the better man would win, whatever the numerical odds. He had defied precedent most of all when before the Battle of the Nile he had trained his fleet captains, his "Band of Brothers," to fight on their own initiative. And the liberty he had taken then had been justified in victory.

If fate should grant him a major battle, Nelson was determined it would be fought upon this new system—a melee in which each ship fought independently. He was a fighter who could think, ready at all times to work at a low margin of safety, not rashly, but with reasoned courage.

By the year 1805, when Nelson had been in the Medi-

Toulon Harbor, shown in the above painting by French artist Joseph Vernet, was the major French base in the Mediterranean. Workmen on shore are arming the ships' cannon.

terranean two years and was beginning to despair of bringing the enemy under his guns, Spain had joined France at war. In the view of Napoleon, who had recently crowned himself Emperor of France, the Spanish alliance afforded a wonderful opportunity to get command of the Channel and launch his veterans across it. He planned ceaselessly. The result was a master scheme by which the fleets at Toulon and Cartagena would elude the British watch, combine, and then make for the Atlantic.

There they would be joined by squadrons from the ports of the Bay of Biscay. Separately or together, the ships would sail toward the West Indies. Then, having wrought havoc among the British West Indian possessions and having taken on fresh supplies, the whole armada would sweep across the Atlantic to the English coast, giving Napoleon the chance he needed to make himself master not merely of the Channel but of the kingdom which lay beyond it.

It was a fine idea—on paper. But it was the dream child of a general, not of a man familiar with the vagaries of wind and sea, of the tasks which faced his admirals, or of the disposition of the enemy. Yet at first fortune favored him. Admiral Villeneuve, who had survived the French defeat at the Nile and was now commanding the fleet at Toulon, did succeed in eluding Nelson in the month of January. He might have made his way to the Atlantic but for the stress of weather.

When Nelson learned of the Admiral's escape, his first thought was that Napoleon had renewed his old idea of the conquest of the East, and he took his battle squadron all the way to Alexandria in search of his opponent. Upon learning that Villeneuve had returned to port, Nelson determined that on the next occasion he would not be drawn so far eastward until he was more certain of the enemy's intentions. He had acted upon a wrong supposition, and he recognized wryly that it was not his own strategic insight but a storm that had foiled the enemy.

Three months later, Villeneuve escaped once more, for a wind which was fair for him at Toulon was unfavorable to the watching frigates. Nor could the frigates, with their few cannon, hope to contest the emergence of a strong enemy detachment. This time the French got clean away, though Villeneuve was so scared of his opponent that he did not stay long enough off Cartagena to join up with the Spaniards.

When at last Nelson knew for certain that Villeneuve's aim was the Atlantic, he met nothing but head winds. He could not make Gibraltar until early in May, by which time the enemy, including ships from Cadiz, had vanished into the unknown. However, after hearing the latest rumors from Gibraltar, Nelson decided the French were making for the West Indies, and on May 11 he headed out across the Atlantic with all possible speed. He arrived off Barbados on

At right are two contemporary British cartoons. Above, four sailors seated on the gun deck of a ship agree that their Nelson is wiser than the biblical King Solomon. Below, John Bull, as a sailor, stands in the Channel and taunts Napoleon, daring him to come out from his fort on the French coast.

June 4, and although he learned that the French fleet was indeed in the vicinity, he was misled by false intelligence into believing that Villeneuve had made for Trinidad. He sped toward that island, hoping to surprise the French unprepared and at anchor, as he had de Brueys at the Nile. He readied his ships for immediate action; but he found nothing.

By the time Nelson had retraced a passage northward, toward Antigua, Villeneuve had learned of his presence. The news so terrified him that he disobeyed Napoleon's orders to wait for the other French ships and took his force straight back to Europe. Nelson had no choice but to follow. When he reached Gibraltar and went ashore it was the first time in almost two years that he had set foot off the *Victory*.

In one vital way, though only one, he was too quick for Villeneuve. With his heavy ships Nelson had no hope of catching the enemy before they returned to home waters, but he sent a fast ship straight to England with the latest news of French movements. He knew that the Admiralty, given the necessary time, would reinforce the fleet that was under Admiral Cornwallis off the mouth of the Channel, and that Cornwallis would make the necessary dispositions to meet the Franco-Spanish squadron.

All went according to Nelson's expectation. Villeneuve was met by a detachment under Admiral Calder off Cape Finisterre on the northwest coast of Spain, but the resultant clash was indecisive. The weather was misty, Calder was in somewhat inferior force, and he was no Nelson. Although he took two Spanish ships of the line, he did not cling to and maul his opponent. He allowed the French to seek refuge in Spanish harbors, where Villeneuve could repair his damage and refresh his men.

Nelson arrived at Gibraltar in the *Victory* a disappointed man. After the long, patient watch, the enemy had been encountered not by him but by Calder. And Calder, who might have drubbed Villeneuve in an open sea-battle, as Jervis did the Spaniards off Cape St. Vincent, was content with a creditable slugging match in the old formal style of fighting. The French lost the engagement, but in Nelsonian terms they remained undefeated.

Having made dispositions to safeguard British interests in the Mediterranean, Nelson steered his course from Gibraltar for England. He was more determined than ever to devise a new plan that would lure the French fleet to its ultimate destruction.

Admiral Calder was recalled because he let the French get away.

Naval Achievements of Great Britain, JENKINS, 1817

This painting of Calder's indecisive engagement shows the British (foreground) keeping their distance from the enemy ships (rear). In the scene at the left, British seamen are getting ready to fire their muzzle-loading cannon once again.

OVERLEAF: *Nelson always hoped to repeat the close-quarters conditions of the Battle of Cape St. Vincent where he had stormed onto the deck of the Spanish San Josef.*

THE TATE GALLERY

VIII

TRAFALGAR

Early one morning, soon after Nelson had reached his beloved estate of Merton, he was greeted by Blackwood, a captain fresh from sea, with the news that Villeneuve had made his way to Cadiz. This was the most welcome news Nelson could have received; it clearly signaled that the French were abandoning their scheme of an attack across the English Channel. Captain Blackwood also reported that Villeneuve's fleet was being watched by Nelson's old friend and long-time comrade-in-arms, Vice Admiral Cuthbert Collingwood.

Almost immediately Nelson was ordered to cancel his leave and return to sea. Being Nelson, he did not hesitate. He was only twenty-five days in England, cheered whenever he was seen in the streets of London, before he started to join Collingwood.

Henry Blackwood later became a vice admiral, but he won fame in 1805 as Nelson's frigate captain.

Villeneuve's withdrawal from the English Channel had removed Napoleon's one last chance of a successful invasion. The French emperor broke up the camps at Boulogne, deciding to use his great army in a land campaign which was to bring him victory at Ulm and Austerlitz, in the heart of the continent. Nelson's immediate duty was therefore no longer in direct defense of his country: it was to destroy the French fleet before it slipped away.

"Friday night, at half-past ten, drove from dear, dear Merton," he wrote in his private diary on September 13, 1805, "where I left all which I hold dear in this world, to go to serve my king and country. May the great God whom I adore enable me to fulfill the expectations of my country; and if it is His good pleasure that I should return, my thanks will never cease being offered up to the throne of His mercy. If it is His good providence to cut short my days

Left, Nelson leaves England for the last time as he boards his barge to join the Victory. *A cheering crowd on the pier is restrained by marines.*

upon earth, I bow with the greatest submission, relying that He will protect those so dear to me that I may leave behind. His will be done. Amen. Amen. Amen."

On September 15, the *Victory* weighed anchor at Spithead, proceeding down the Channel in company with Blackwood's ship, the *Euryalus*, the smartest frigate in the navy. It was fitting that the commander in chief and his leading cruiser captain should sail together: Blackwood, the eyes of the fleet; Nelson, its brains and spirit. On September 28, the day before his forty-seventh birthday, Nelson resumed command of the British ships off Europe's southwestern coast.

He transformed everything. Collingwood threw off the care which had begun to fatigue him and was glad to serve under a friend he respected. Their methods differed: Collingwood believed in a close watch, Nelson in a distant one. Collingwood's discipline was strict, while Nelson's was less so, but they trusted one another, and in their hearts they were united.

The fleet was made up of varied elements. Some ships were from Nelson's original squadron. Some had served with Calder in his action off Finisterre; some were newly joined from home. Such diverse material needed welding into a unit, and Nelson was the one man likely to be able to do this quickly.

Nelson intended to stand well away into the Atlantic, leaving the business of observation to Blackwood and his frigates, which would signal enemy movements as soon as they were apparent.

Meanwhile, there was a master plan to explain to the captains. This was issued as a formal memorandum to each commanding officer, but Nelson expounded it in person, generally over dinner in his cabin or in conversation afterward.

Captain Keats of the *Superb*, who was unlucky enough to miss serving off Cadiz, although he had done well in the pursuit of Villeneuve to the West Indies, had been given the gist of the idea in England, and he noted it down with all the excitement with which it must have struck him. It was something new in naval warfare.

"One day," wrote Keats, "walking with Lord Nelson in the grounds at Merton, talking on naval matters, he said to me: 'No day can be long enough to arrange a couple of fleets, and fight a decisive battle, according to the old system. When we meet them (I was to have been with him), for meet them we shall, I'll tell you how I shall fight them.

TEXT CONTINUED ON PAGE 128

Nelson's favorite picture of Emma Hamilton, left, was painted in 1800 by Johann Schmidt. It hung in Nelson's cabin on the Victory. *Part of his last letter to Emma, below, was discovered after Trafalgar. She added the note, which reads: "This letter was found open on His desk and brought to Lady Hamilton by Capt. Hardy. Oh miserable and wretched Emma. Oh glorious and happy Nelson."*

THE NELSON TOUCH

When Nelson explained his plan (above) for the coming battle, his captains wept with joy and anticipation, hailing the "Nelson touch." The objective of the plan was to pierce the line of the combined French and Spanish fleets in two or three places by sailing directly at it rather than by cruising down alongside it. Yet this meant that the leading British ships would be exposed to the full power of the enemy's broadsides, without being able to bring their own guns to bear. When the battle began (see diagram), two British squadrons headed by Nelson and Collingwood were aimed like arrows toward the three-mile-long enemy column. Collingwood's ship, the Royal Sovereign, *broke through first, shortly after noon. Nelson's* Victory, *followed by ten other ships, closed with the enemy more than half an hour later. In the background of the view at right is Spain's Cape Trafalgar.*

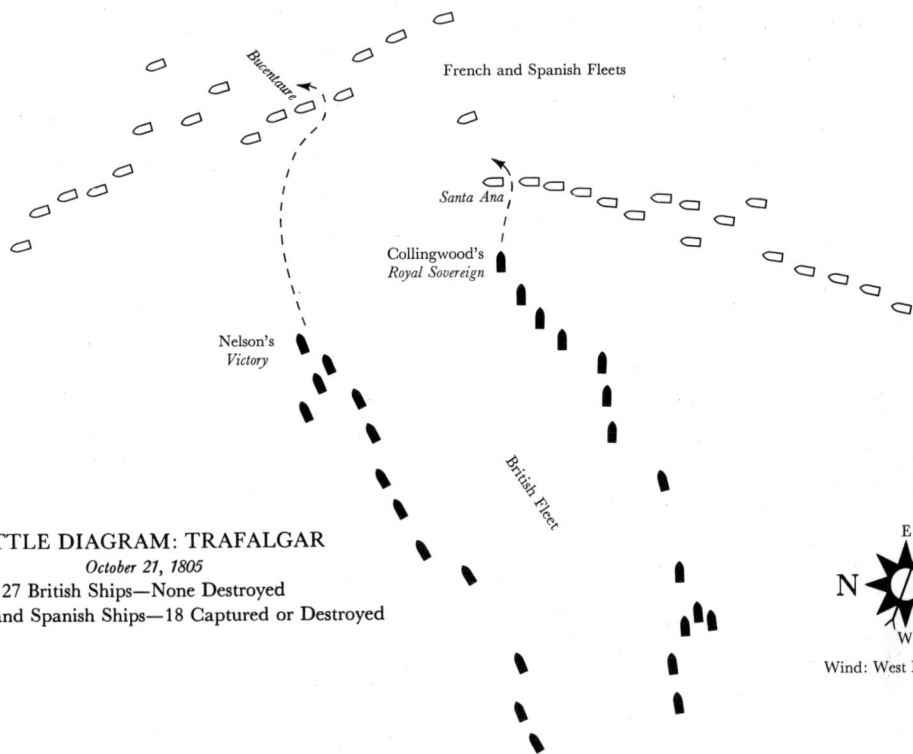

BATTLE DIAGRAM: TRAFALGAR
October 21, 1805
27 British Ships—None Destroyed
33 French and Spanish Ships—18 Captured or Destroyed

French and Spanish Fleets

Bucentaure

Santa Ana

Collingwood's
Royal Sovereign

Nelson's
Victory

British Fleet

Wind: West North West

TEXT CONTINUED FROM PAGE 124

" 'I shall form the fleet into three divisions in three lines. One division shall be composed of twelve or fourteen of the fastest two-decked ships, which I shall always keep to windward, or in a situation of advantage; and I shall put them under an officer who, I am sure, will employ them in the manner I wish, if possible. I consider it will always be in my power to throw them into battle in any part I may choose; but if circumstances prevent their being carried against the enemy where I desire, I shall feel certain he will employ them effectually, and perhaps in a more advantageous manner than if he could have followed my orders.

" 'With the remaining part of the fleet formed in two lines, I shall go at them at once, if I can, about one third of their line from the leading ship.' He then said, 'What do you think of it?' Such a question I felt required consideration. I paused. Seeing it, he said, 'But I'll tell you what I think of it! I think it will surprise and confound the enemy. They won't know what I am about. It will bring forward a pell-mell battle, and that is what I want!' ''

Villeneuve (right) was to be Nelson's opponent. Ships of both fleets were similar, but French design was more graceful. Below are a French frigate, a tender, and a prison ship.

BIBLIOTHEQUE NATIONALE

Iconographic Encyclopedia, HECK, 1851

In the British cartoon above, Sailor Jack kneels beside a gun to pray that the cannon shot may be distributed the same as the prize money—the most among the officers. Copies of caricatures such as this one were displayed in city shop-windows and sold by print sellers. They usually lampooned political situations and well-known personalties of the time.

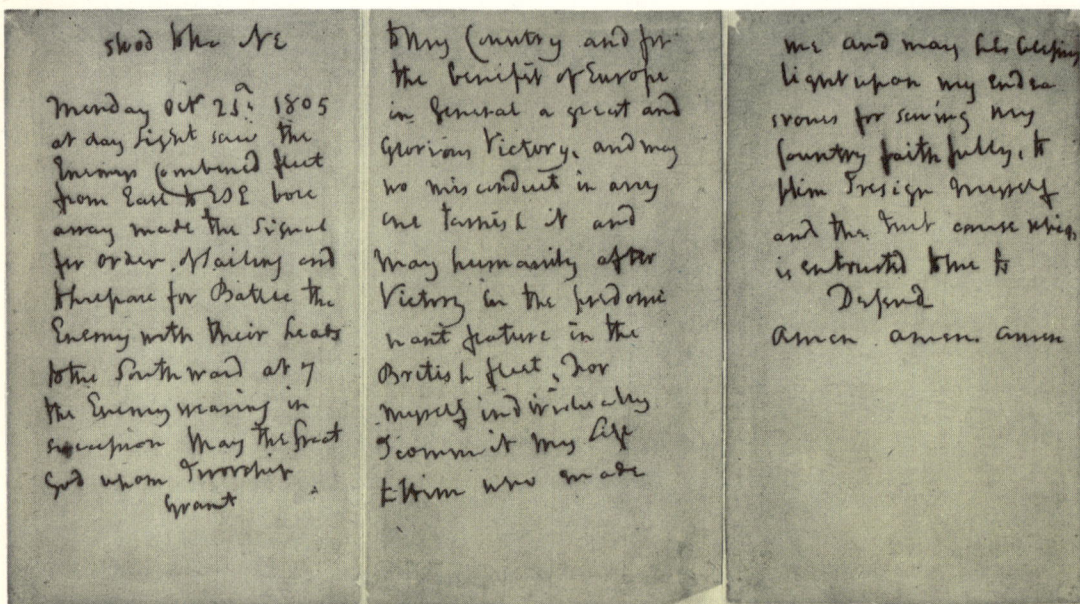

Before the start of the action, Nelson withdrew to the privacy of his cabin to write this prayer in his own diary.

These words with Keats not only had the core of the matter, but Keats' record had caught something of Nelson's own enthusiasm, which had the effect upon his captains of an electric shock.

When the time came, Nelson did not have enough ships to form his fast, detached first division at all, but his plan of an approach "in two lines," head on, to accomplish the disruption of enemy formations, brought about exactly the result he intended. "Some shed tears," said Nelson when he described the effect of his plan upon his officers, "all approved. It was new, it was singular, it was simple!" "It must succeed," said the captains off Cadiz, "if ever they will allow us to go at them." It was no wonder that Nelson described his reception in the fleet as "causing the sweetest sensation of my life."

Many experienced officers, including Fremantle, who now commanded the three-decked *Neptune*, did not believe that Villeneuve would dare to venture out of port. The season was growing late, and he could stay snug the whole winter. Nelson thought differently. And Napoleon played straight into his hands, first by ordering Villeneuve into the Mediterranean at the earliest opportunity, and then by sending a senior admiral to relieve him. The insult was too much for Villeneuve to bear—he had to retrieve his reputation by fighting. On October 19, after Nelson had been given a few essential weeks to shape his fleet, Blackwood reported that the French and the Spaniards were preparing to sail.

Villeneuve had in fact ordered part of his force to drive Blackwood away, together with the other inshore British ships. The scheme had not succeeded; but since the captains concerned in that operation could not return to Cadiz because of an offshore wind, Villeneuve had no choice but to sail out with his whole force. Villeneuve was willing to be bold because he believed that Nelson had detached a number of ships to provision at Gibraltar, and also because he knew that in any case he had but a few days longer in which to exercise command. The news of British ships provisioning was true, but Nelson still had twenty-seven of the line with him. Villeneuve had thirty-three, of which fifteen were Spanish.

When Nelson had news that the enemy was stirring, he was well out to sea. He ordered his ships to steer at once for the Strait of Gibraltar, intending to deny the enemy passage into the Mediterranean.

The night of October 19 and the day and night of the

During a moment of solitude before the clash, Nelson kneels in prayer.

As the great naval fleets neared each other, Nelson ordered that a signal be flown to "amuse" his men. At right is the order of the flags as they appeared, spelling out ENGLAND EXPECTS THAT EVERY MAN WILL DO HIS DUTY. *Nelson, at center in the picture above, watches the message being raised. Until the ships closed for action, seamen cheered and bands played.*

20th were taken up with maneuvers. Villeneuve was struggling, not with entire success, to get his ships into regular formation, while Nelson kept his main striking force out of sight long enough so that his opponent would be fully committed to the plan of carrying out his orders by sailing through the Strait.

At first light on October 21, the fleets sighted each other, just off the coast of Spain's Cape Trafalgar. Nelson signaled for his ships to dispose themselves in two columns, according to his plan: the windward under his own command, the leeward under that of Collingwood. Such wind as there was blew toward the enemy, as Nelson would have hoped.

At about eight o'clock or a little earlier, Villeneuve reversed course, an action which Nelson had anticipated. His purpose was to retreat upon Cadiz. As it was now impossible for the French and the Spaniards to reach Gibraltar without a major battle, the move was sound. Whatever the result of the fight with Nelson, which was now unavoidable, Villeneuve could at least repair his damage afterward.

TEXT CONTINUED ON PAGE 138

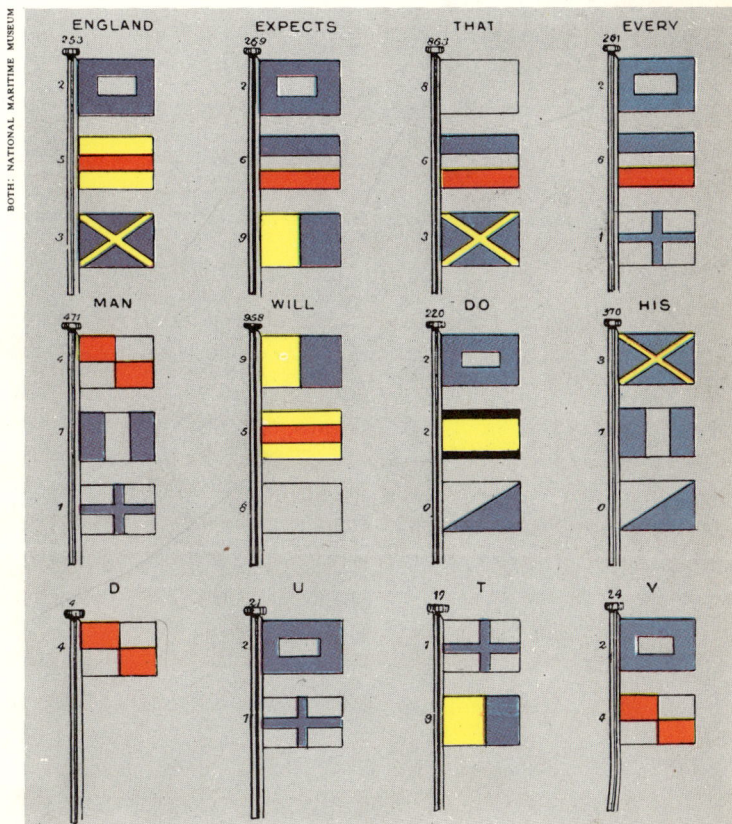

ENGLAND EXPECTS THAT EVERY
MAN WILL DO HIS
D U T V

133

OTH: *Naval Achievements of Great Britain*, JENKINS, 1817

THROUGH THE SMOKE
OF BATTLE

At first there was a plan and an order to the Battle of Trafalgar. Nelson's Victory *sliced through the enemy line at precisely the right point (above), just astern of Admiral Villeneuve's* Bucentaure. *This cut off the northern portion of the enemy column and allowed Collingwood's squadron to overwhelm the southern part. At left, the French* Achille *burns to her waterline, having been blasted by Collingwood's ships. But as the blinding yellow smoke of battle rolled across the waters, opponents had to be taken on in any order they came; this was the kind of pell-mell battle that Nelson had wanted. It brought out the best in men of his stripe—the worst in others. Admiral Dumanoir, the French commander of the northernmost enemy ships (above left), fled toward Cadiz after exchanging only a few shots.*

OVERLEAF: *In this painting Turner gives his impression of Trafalgar, with the* Victory *surrounded by drowning sailors and battle debris.*

GREENWICH HOSPITAL COLLECTION

135

TEXT CONTINUED FROM PAGE 133

Although the wind was light, there was a swell from the west which gave Nelson the idea—justified by events —that there would be a gale before nightfall, or at latest the next day. The advance toward the enemy was slow, never more than a walking pace, though every ship crowded on sail. There was much to say and do, and time to do it in. One of Nelson's first acts was to summon the frigate captains aboard the *Victory* to give them final instructions. These amounted to no more than that they were to tell succeeding ships to get into action as best they could, without regard to any regular order of sailing.

Captains Blackwood and Hardy were called to Nelson's day cabin to witness a codicil to his will in which he entrusted Emma Hamilton to the care of his country. Nelson then went the rounds of the ship, praising Hardy's arrangements. Afterward he withdrew to his quarters where Pasco, the signal lieutenant, later found him on his knees. He was committing a prayer to his private diary. It was found after the battle, and it is one which has passed into the treasury of the English language.

"May the great God, whom I worship, grant to my country, and for the benefit of Europe in general, a great and glorious victory; and may no misconduct in anyone tarnish it; and may humanity after victory be the predominant feature in the British fleet. For myself, individually, I commit my life to Him who made me, and may His blessing light upon my endeavors for serving my country faithfully. To Him I resign myself and the just cause which is entrusted to me to defend. Amen. Amen. Amen."

When Nelson returned to the upper deck, he said to Blackwood: "I'll now amuse the fleet," asking his friend if he did not think there was a signal still wanting. Blackwood replied No, he was sure that everyone knew exactly what they were about. Nevertheless, Nelson kept to his opinion, and he said to the signal lieutenant, "Mr. Pasco, I wish to say to the fleet, ENGLAND CONFIDES THAT EVERY MAN WILL DO HIS DUTY," and he added, "You must be quick, for I have one more to make, which is for close action." Pasco then asked if he could substitute "expects" for "confides" because the first word was in the signal book and "confides" would have to be spelled. Nelson replied with seeming satisfaction, "That will do, Pasco, make it directly."

TEXT CONTINUED ON PAGE 142

During the battle, an approaching storm caused huge swells to rock the fighting ships. Right, the Victory *rolls heavily as the storm comes on at sunset.*

A view of the Victory's main deck at the height of battle. French sharpshooters in the rigging of the Redoubtable

...t wounded Nelson (right center). Other men are falling as the gun crews fire the cannon and marines sight their muskets.

TEXT CONTINUED FROM PAGE 138

It was thus that the ships went into action, with the signal flying from the halyards of the *Victory*, with bands playing until action was joined, and with a white ensign flown in every ship. There were those in the fleet who thought the message superfluous. Collingwood, for instance, said he wished Nelson would stop signaling, since everyone would do his duty as a matter of course. What were they there for? But when Napoleon heard of it later, he ordered a similar message to be painted on all his ships of war: "*La France Compte que chacun fera son Devoir.*"

Nelson was taking a grave personal risk in order to get into action quickly. It was against all reason—and precedent—that the *Victory* should lead her line, particularly in an action where the foremost ships were bound to suffer heavily. They were approaching the enemy bows-on and would be unable to bring their broadsides to bear until they had closed. Blackwood, Hardy, and other senior officers were so concerned for Nelson's safety that at one time they actually persuaded him to let the second ship, the *Temeraire*, overtake the *Victory*. But when the moment came, Nelson changed his mind and ordered her captain to keep her in station astern.

Unconcerned for himself, Nelson grew agitated when Collingwood, in the *Royal Sovereign*, leading his own line, was seen to be exposing himself in exactly the same way. Nelson actually signaled to one of the 74-gun ships to overtake the admiral and get into action before him.

But Collingwood was as obstinate as Nelson. He continued to crowd on sail, and remained far ahead of the rest of his column, for the *Royal Sovereign* was as good a sailer as the *Victory*. Collingwood got into action about noon. For some time he fought alone, until succeeding ships, approaching slowly in the light airs, and suffering much in their rigging from enemy fire, could bring him support.

Nelson's column did not get into close action until about half an hour after Collingwood's, and then for the rest of that crowded October day, every vessel became involved in that "pell-mell battle" which Nelson had brought about.

The struggle was fierce and costly, particularly among the leading British ships. But when the day closed, at least eighteen Frenchmen and Spaniards had struck their colors, though not all of them had actually been boarded and secured. By breaking Villeneuve's line in two places, Nelson had isolated groups of enemy ships, battering them into submission before help could come. The way of attack was,

Wounded, Nelson was carried to the cockpit (above). Hardy stands over him; Dr. Beatty feels his pulse, and another doctor rubs his chest to ease his pain. Nelson died knowing that victory was assured.

in effect, the Nile in reverse. In that battle, the French rear was made impotent because it could not join the action; at Trafalgar, the leading enemy ships were excluded. In the conditions of the day it took a long time to turn, and by the time the leading ships could join they were too late.

The most unorthodox sea victory of the age of sail had been won in the space of about four hours, and Nelson had achieved his wish. As a fleet, Villeneuve's combined force had been broken beyond recovery. The gale which Nelson had foreseen, bringing havoc with it, had robbed the victors of all but four of their prizes, but no British ship was lost, and Villeneuve, together with his entire staff, became a prisoner of war. Napoleon never forgave his admiral, who

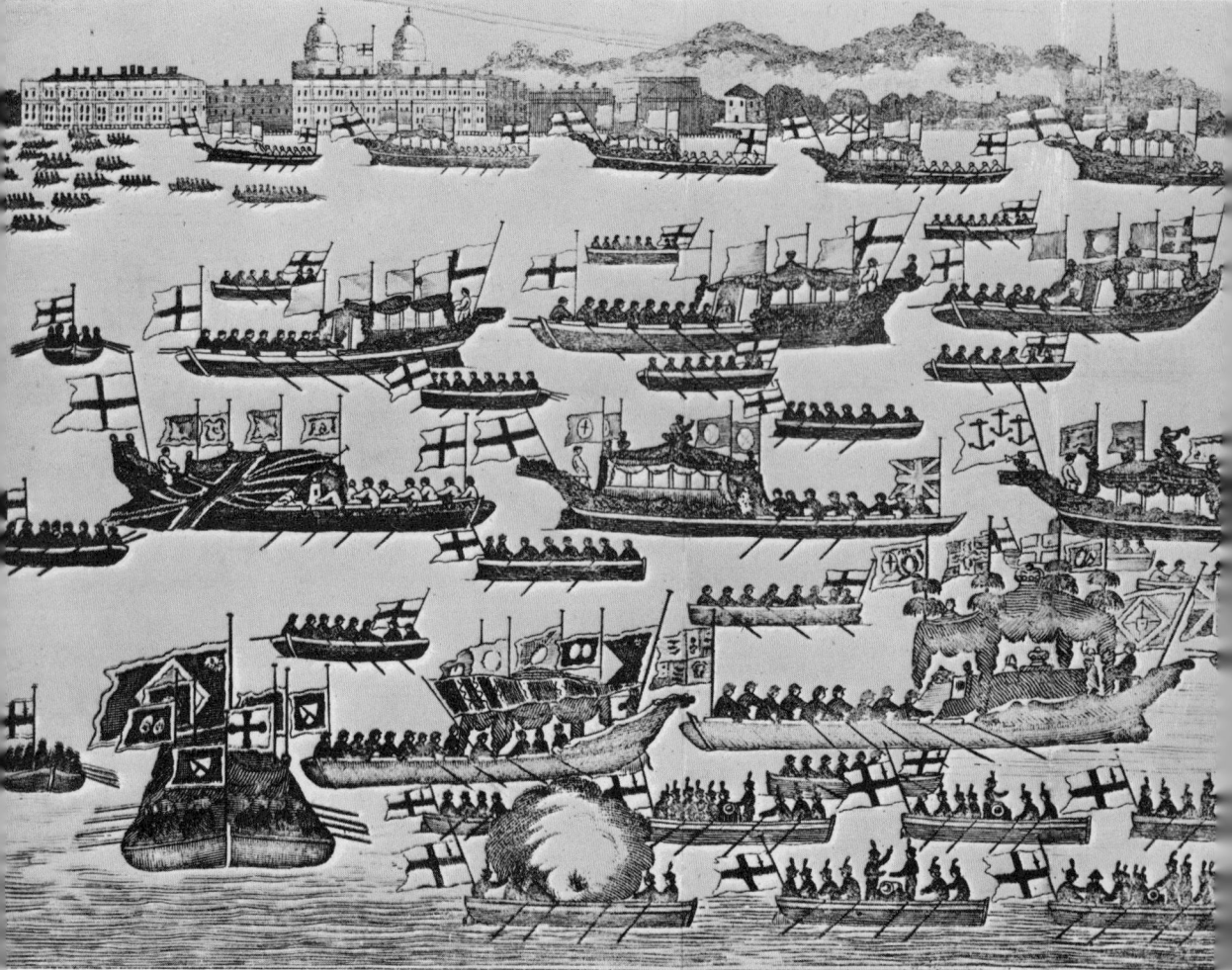

died, in disgrace, within a few months of the action. But before the battle ended in triumph for the British, tragedy struck.

About 1:15, as he was pacing around the quarter-deck with Hardy, Nelson was hit by a bullet from a marksman in the French *Redoubtable*, a ship which was splendidly handled by Lucas, her captain. "They have done for me at last, Hardy," said Nelson as he fell. "My backbone is shot through." He was carried below by a sergeant of marines and a party of seamen, his face covered with a handkerchief so that the men should not be discouraged by the sight of their wounded admiral.

Nelson lingered for three hours, in great pain, but he lived to hear from Hardy the news he longed for, and he then bade his friend kiss him in farewell. His own line had achieved its aim of preventing the French from interfering with Collingwood, while Collingwood had dealt faithfully with the rear of the French and Spanish columns. Between them the admirals had set a standard for all time, not only of tactics but of personal conduct. Every circumstance had conspired to make the day one of the most dramatic in naval annals.

Having done his duty, as he said so openly and so thankfully during his last hours, Nelson could die content, and at the time of his supreme fulfillment. Of the many records of his death, none in its own way is more characteristic and complete than the formal words entered in the flagship's log.

"Partial firing continued until 4:30, when a victory having been reported to the Right Honorable Lord Viscount Nelson, K.B. and Commander in Chief, he then died of his wound."

Nelson's life was given to a single end, which was to make his country great by means of her navy. He succeeded. His navy remained predominant for more than a century, and when at last it yielded place, it was to the navy of America, a nation nurtured on the same traditions.

The essence of Nelson's leadership was that he could inspire everyone around him to excel themselves; and of all the great men in what was, without doubt, a heroic age, he was the man to command love.

Nelson's impact on his own profession cannot be illustrated better than by relating an incident in a battle fought near Lissa in the Adriatic Sea. It took place six years after Trafalgar and it was won by Commodore Sir William Hoste, a pupil of Nelson's who defeated a superior force in a running fight. Hoste was a Norfolk man; he had in fact first been taken to sea in the *Agamemnon*. He hero-worshiped Nelson and had distinguished himself in many of his engagements.

One of the captains at Lissa wrote home to his father after the battle to say that "The only signals our Commodore made were to form the line of battle, and then a telegraphic message, 'Remember Nelson.'

"It would be very difficult for me at all to convey to you any idea of the sensation with which these words appeared to affect our men, but there was something finer in it than words can express. Before, the men had been all animation, cheering each other's ships as we passed, but the instant the signal was made known to them, you might have heard a pin drop, and though with almost tears in their eyes, their countenances manifested such a spirit of determination as nothing could overcome. It was worth a thousand cheers, and never again as long as I live shall I see so interesting or so glorious a moment."

Nelson has been remembered ever since. His body lies in St. Paul's Cathedral, in a coffin made from the mainmast of *L'Orient*, the flagship of Admiral de Brueys at the Battle of the Nile. His last stately home, the *Victory*, lies in dock at Portsmouth, a place of pilgrimage to those of every nation who feel the force of example. His statue dominates London's Trafalgar Square, and it faces toward the sea.

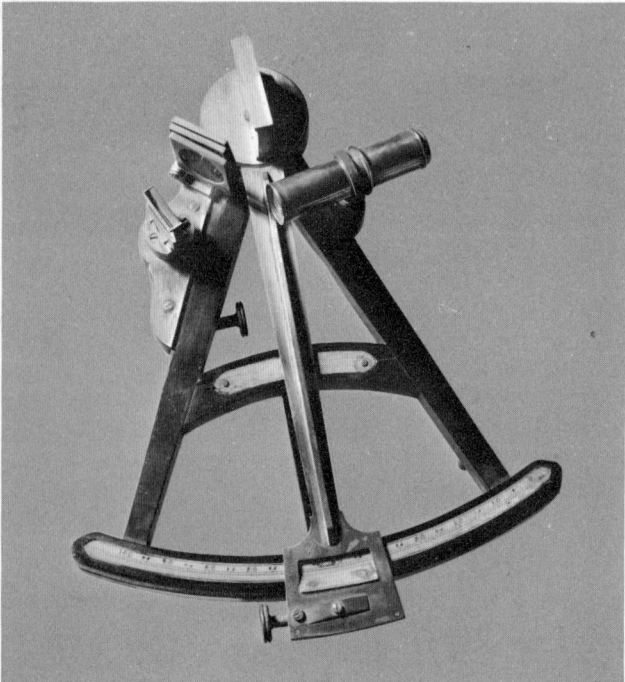

The Nelson Column was erected in Trafalgar Square in 1843. At right, it overlooks the city of London today. The statue of Nelson at the top is seventeen feet high. One of many Nelson relics is his quadrant (left).

After his death, pictures of Nelson were in great demand. His image appeared on tankards, jugs, and other humble objects. These enamel snuff boxes are now valuable museum items.

AMERICAN HERITAGE PUBLISHING CO., INC.

BOOK DIVISION
RICHARD M. KETCHUM, *Editor*

HORIZON CARAVEL BOOKS
RUSSELL BOURNE, *Editor*

MERVYN D. KAUFMAN, *Assistant Editor*

JUDITH HARKISON, *Chief Picture Researcher*

LUCY DAVIDSON, *Picture Researcher*

ELAINE K. ANDREWS, *Copy Editor*

JANET CZARNETZKI, *Art Director*

GERTRUDIS FELIU, *Chief, European Bureau*

MAUREEN GREEN, *European Bureau*

ACKNOWLEDGMENTS

The Editors are deeply indebted to the staff members of many private and public collections in which paintings, photographs, and articles of special importance to this book were found. Foremost among these collections are the National Maritime Museum, Greenwich, England, and the Greenwich Hospital Collection, on permanent loan to the National Maritime Museum; the Victory Museum, Portsmouth Dockyard, Portsmouth, England; and the Prints Division, New York Public Library. In addition, the Editors wish to thank the following individuals and organizations for their assistance and for making available material in their collections:

Michael S. Robinson, Edward Archibald, Miss P. Sichel —Prints and Drawings Department, National Maritime Museum

George P. B. Naish—Keeper of Models, Draughts, and Relics of the National Maritime Museum

Instructor Captain T. E. Jackson—Curator of the Victory

Museum, Portsmouth Dockyard

Lieutenant B. A. Hill, R.N.—the *Victory*, Portsmouth Dockyard

Lieutenant Colonel Harold Wyllie, O.B.E.—Perthshire, Scotland

Sir Bruce Ingram—London

Special research and photography: New York—Geoffrey Clements; England—Zoltan Wegner, Brian Seed, John Freeman, Alan Clifton; Italy—Maria Todorow, Maria Giulia Rispoli, Giulio Parisio
Special drawings by Colin Mudie, A.M.R.I.N.A.

FURTHER REFERENCE

Readers interested in further examining the art and artifacts of the Nelson era will find collections of varying kinds in the National Maritime Museum, Greenwich, and in the Victory Museum at Portsmouth Dockyard, England. For general naval material of the period, there are several collections in American cities. Some of the most important exhibits open to the public are the Mariners Museum in Newport News, Va.; the U.S. Naval Academy Museum, Annapolis, Md.; the Division of Naval History, Smithsonian Institution; Mystic Seaport, Mystic, Conn.; the Irving S. Olds Collection, New York City; the Franklin D. Roosevelt Library, Hyde Park, N.Y.; and the Peabody Museum, Salem, Mass.

For those who wish to read more about Nelson and his navy, the following books are recommended:

Beresford, Charles. *Nelson and His Times*. Harmsworth Bros. Ltd., 1898.

Bowen, Frank C. *The Sea*. Halton & Truscott Smith, 1925.

Britton, C. *New Chronicles of the Life of Lord Nelson*. Cornish Bros., 1947.

Callender, Geoffrey. *The Life of Nelson*. Longmans, Green, 1912.

Forester, C. S. *Lord Nelson*. Bobbs-Merrill, 1929.

Grenfell, Russell. *Nelson the Sailor*. Faber & Faber, 1949.

Hadden, James. *The Boy's Life of Nelson*. S. W. Partridge Co., 1908.

Kennedy, Ludovic. *Nelson's Captains*. Norton Co., 1951.

Lloyd, Christopher. *Ships and Seamen*. World, 1961.

Mahan, A. T. *Nelson at Naples*. Spottiswoode & Co., 1900; *The Influence of Sea Power Upon History 1660–1783*. Hill

and Wang, 1957; *The Life of Nelson*. Little, Brown, 1943.

Maine, Rene. *Trafalgar*. Scribner's, 1957.

Naish, George P. B. *Nelson's Letters to His Wife*. Navy Records Society, England, 1958.

Nimitz, Chester W. and Potter, E. B. *Sea Power*. Prentice Hall, 1960.

Oman, Carola. *Nelson*. Doubleday, 1946.

Pope, Dudley. *Decision at Trafalgar*. Lippincott, 1960.

Sherrard, O. A. *A Life of Emma Hamilton*. Sidgewick & Jackson Ltd., 1927.

Warner, Oliver. *A Portrait of Lord Nelson*. Chatto & Windus, 1958; *The Battle of the Nile*. Macmillan, 1960; *Victory: The Life of Lord Nelson*. Little, Brown, 1958.

Williamson, James. *The English Channel*. World, 1959.

This faithful model of the Victory *is in the National Maritime Museum in Greenwich, England.*

INDEX

Bold face indicates pages on which maps or illustrations appear

Iconographic Encyclopedia, HECK, 1851